The Family Link to Education

The Family Link to Education

The Road to Personal and Professional Success

Rex A. Holiday and Steve Sonntag

ROWMAN & LITTLEFIELD
Lanham • Boulder • New York • London

Published by Rowman & Littlefield
An imprint of The Rowman & Littlefield Publishing Group, Inc.
4501 Forbes Boulevard, Suite 200, Lanham, Maryland 20706
www.rowman.com

Unit A, Whitacre Mews, 26-34 Stannary Street, London SE11 4AB

British Library Cataloguing in Publication Information Available

Library of Congress Cataloging-in-Publication Data Available

ISBN: 978-1-4758-4516-7 (cloth : alk. paper)
ISBN: 978-1-4758-4517-4 (electronic)

∞ ™ The paper used in this publication meets the minimum requirements of American
National Standard for Information Sciences—Permanence of Paper for Printed Library
Materials, ANSI/NISO Z39.48-1992.

Printed in the United States of America

Contents

Acknowledgments

REX A. HOLIDAY, PHD

I would like to dedicate "The Family," part I of *The Family Link to Education: The Road to Personal and Professional Success*, to my wife and eternal companion, Jane Faith Holiday. She has sacrificed so much for me and our children, and if it had not been for her constant encouragement I would not have been successful in most of my major accomplishments, including completing this collaborative book project. I guess you can say that it is in her middle name.

I thank my mother, Lila Holiday, for instinctively knowing that talking, reading, and singing would help develop my young mind and intellect. Mom was always so patient with me when I would repeat, more than once, "Read it again, Mommy!" Of course she always did, and I always loved it.

I thank my father, Charlie Holiday, who, although tragically gone by the age of forty-two, left an everlasting impression on me about the importance of education. Dad taught industrial arts and math at the secondary school level in the Sequoia Unified School District located in Redwood City, California. At the time of his death, Dad was enrolled in graduate school at San Jose State University pursuing a Master of Science degree in chemistry.

I want to thank my sister, Robbin Holiday-Lawson, for her dedication to teaching STEM at the secondary and postsecondary level for more than two decades. I also want to thank my sister Rita Holiday, who works in public relations for a Silicon Valley technology giant where she promotes STEM for women and girls through scholarships and mentoring programs.

I want to thank my grandparents, great-grandparents, and great-great-grandparents who passed down a legacy of teaching from one generation to the next on my mother's and on my father's sides of the family. While as of this writing I have never formally taught in the classroom, I am convinced that teaching is in my genes.

I thank my friend, Dale Fritchen, who encouraged me to take a seat on the Manteca Unified School District (MUSD) board of trustees. I also want to thank the MUSD administrators for their continued support with all of my research in education projects.

Finally, I thank my Heavenly Father for blessing me with an amazing spouse, experiences, opportunities, and the intellect required to cowrite this book.

STEVE SONNTAG

I wish to dedicate *The Family Link to Education: The Road to Personal and Professional Success* to my parents, Lewis L. Sonntag and Natalie R. Sonntag, and to the rest of my relatives, especially to my maternal grandmother, Rebecca Yaspan, who literally saved my life, gave me personal attention and love, and really was the mentor who originally inspired me to teach.

During my school years, my school counselor, Mr. Osegueda; my Spanish teachers, Mr. Harvey, Mrs. Cannon, and Dr. Galán; and the international program director, Dr. Lantos, were particularly helpful and encouraging. It was because of their sincerity to students and their dedication to the school community that I also chose to become a teacher. Indeed, they were great role models for others as well as for me.

My personal friends, the Ballew family, Woody Brown, Miklos Fejer, Mike Forman, Arlene Krauss, Thu Lam, Leo and Aziza Mara, Michelle and Giovanna Mercurio, Christian Mitchell, Jordan Mitchell, the O'Leary family, the Shalom-Nautico Community, Karen Steves-Ott, and Adele Stinson are very loving and very supportive and have helped me both personally and professionally. Jerry Hackett and his philosophy of being "self-full" in order to become better personally have been especially helpful for me.

My professional friends, Dr. Edward Brasmer, Marcia Chapman, Carol De Sá Campos, Mindie Dolson, Denise Elling, Sarah Fox, Jeff Gaines, Terri Godinez, Barbara Henry, Bill Jones, Joe Mora, Nina Norton, Bonna Purdy, and Jim Stoker, have been exceptionally wonderful role models for so many people as well as for myself.

I also extend my professional acknowledgment to Bertram Linder, the educational literary agent who guided me with my previous books for teachers and for families and who has unfortunately passed.

Along with all of my former students, since retiring I have had the pleasure of working with other students, with their parents, and with adults who are also very inspirational, intelligent, and humble. Those particular people have been Allie, Alyssa, Annie, Beau, Connor, David, Davis, Derek, Dylan, Erin, Katie, Laura, Lauren, Lexy, Lia, Margaret, Matthew, Miya, Patrick, Salima, Sarah, Shane, Sofia, Tiffany, and Yasmin.

Jenna is a unique young lady whose perspective about life is very positive, and she is very humble. Her attitude and her personality are truly allowing her to achieve all of her goals in her life while being an outstanding role model for her family, friends, and everyone else whom she encounters.

To all of you whom I honor in this acknowledgment, thank you for being you. I admire all of you immensely.

I

The Family

Introduction to Part I: The Family

Rex A. Holiday, PhD

It has been said that no amount of success outside of the home can compensate for failure inside of the home. The saying is all-inclusive, and does not point to any specific individual. Failure inside of the home affects each and every member of the family in some way or another. Likewise, success outside of the home will also have some residual effect on every family member. In most circumstances, a strong home foundation is a prerequisite to success outside of the home.

The term *family*, as it is used in this book, denotes a general concept of family, but it is not meant to define what a family is or what a family should be. Families come in a variety of shapes, sizes, and parent-child dynamics, so in order to avoid the perception of exclusivity or naiveté, this book purposely exposes some of its own assumptions about families. Some of the unique dynamics in families include socioeconomic status, education level, single or divorced parents, special needs children, or even special needs parents.

There are also homes where children are raised by grandparents, foster parents, uncles and aunts, or even their older siblings. The hope is that no matter the family structure, the advice and suggestions of each chapter and subsection will provide information that can be adapted to each family's unique situation.

The intellectual and social foundations that children receive at home are more traditionally referred to as *nurturing*, and nurturing at home typically involves *physical, emotional, intellectual*, and *spiritual* components. To nurture is to fulfill a need. For example, infants rely on parents to meet their physical needs, but *communication*—both *tactile* and *verbal*—is just as vital

3

in the infant phase as it is for older children. As children grow and become more aware, parental nurturing begins to fulfill their emotional, intellectual, and spiritual needs.

The first concept to be explored in part I, "The Family," is a chapter entitled "Family Nurturing," and it is broken into four subsections:

• Nurturing Tactile and Verbal Communication
• Nurturing Emotions
• Nurturing the Intellect
• Nurturing Self-Awareness and Potential

These subsections are meant to be a catalyst for the critical thinking that parents and guardians often have to use in order to understand how to address the mental, physical, emotional, and spiritual needs of their children.

In chapter 2, "Life Lessons Learned Within the Family," the focus is on the knowledge gained from being taught by those who are chiefly responsible for child-rearing and from incidental experiences in the home. In most families the first lessons taught are the *do*s and *don't*s with regard to what is established as acceptable and unacceptable behavior. The latter are particularly critical to establish in a child's early developmental years because they teach children about choices and the consequences that result from the choices they make. The subsections are broken down into the following categories:

• Rules—Why We Have Them and Why We Follow Them
• Focus On the *Dos* But Understand the *Don't*s
• Family Relations

Family hierarchies are also discussed in order to show how authority is established within the family structure.

Chapter 3, "Family History," discusses the essence of what family history means. Three subcategories are used to present a broader view of the family history phenomenon:

• Ancestors—What Can You Learn From Them?
• Culture—Who You Are and Why That Matters
• Family Traditions—Make Good Ones and Preserve Them

The lessons to be learned from those who came before can either help present and future generations avoid pitfalls or repeat successes. It is also important for family members to know who they are based on their ancestry because it helps them to understand the *culture* from which their parents, grandparents, and great-grandparents were molded. Once they understand their culture, they are more able to understand family traditions and why they are important.

Building upon what is learned from the chapters on life lessons and family history, chapter 4, "Family Legacy," shows how what is taught within the family dynamic, such as knowing that *choices* bring *consequences* (positive and negative), is only the beginning. Furthermore, the chapter shows that the next step is to understand why some choices bring positive consequences while others bring negative consequences. The latter will help children throughout their lives because understanding the nature of choices (that is, that they bring consequences) can compel them to make good ones. The following are the subcategories for this chapter:

• Family Philosophy—Why We Think the Way We Think
• Serving Others First
• Creating and Maintaining a Positive Image

These subsections are meant to reveal to parents and guardians what some of the potential consequences are for what is taught in the home regarding attitudes and assumptions about others based on race, religion, political affiliation, socioeconomic status, gender, and all of the other characteristics and traits that make up who and what people are. Just as one of the quotes in the "Family Legacy" chapter implies, what we learn at home has profound effects on how we perceive the world, and for that reason it is imperative that we teach in the home the importance of looking for the good in everyone and in every situation.

Technology and how it can be used to bridge the generation gaps within the family is the focus and topic of the final chapter of part I, "Family and the Technology Gap." In what is best described as a reversal of mentor-protégé roles between parent and child, the latter appear to take the leadership role in most cases when it comes to using the latest technology. Due to the speed at which technology evolves, there is a technology gap that broadens with each generation.

The *technology gap* causes many parents to be intimidated by digital technology, but it is imperative that parents learn how to use the latest technology in order to better determine which technologies are beneficial for their children and which are not. It is also imperative that the digitally illiterate become digitally literate because there exists a danger of becoming technologically extinct.

Chapter One

Family Nurturing

As infants and young children, most people are fortunate enough to have their basic needs—such as food and shelter—provided by mothers or someone who has been given that responsibility. It does not take a research study to determine what the result will be if food and shelter are not provided for infants and young children, but there are other vital needs that are not as obvious. One example is *tactile communication.*

NURTURING TACTILE AND VERBAL COMMUNICATION

Long before a child learns to communicate verbally, they familiarize themselves with the world around them by using their five senses: sight, hearing, smell, taste, and touch. Primary among these for infants are smell, taste, and touch. It is not by accident that Helen Keller, the famed public speaker (hearing- and sight-impaired since infancy), learned to communicate verbally by mastering her smell, taste, and touch senses. Even for infants who are not vision- or hearing-impaired, smell, taste, and touch are the senses they rely on most.

Before children are able to focus visually and audibly, it is crucial that they have constant communication through smell, taste, and touch; as demonstrated with the example of Helen Keller, smell, taste, and touch are the most important senses for learning in the early stages of development. Occupational therapist Cassy Christianson says, "Newborns can't hear certain very quiet sounds" and "can focus on objects about eight to 15 inches away"; however, smell, taste, and touch are fully developed senses at birth (2014).

Most preschool instruction involves some element of learning by familiarizing children with their five senses, and, over time, some children will develop a proclivity for tactile learning while others will be more prone to auditory or visual learning. According to educator and classroom technology specialist Boni Hamilton (2015), students in the early grades prefer more hands-on exercises, but some of the same students will lose interest in hands-on type learning in the upper grade levels. Implicit in the latter observation is that there is a small window of opportunity to take advantage of a tactile learning engagement.

Effective verbal communication is one of the most important skills a child will ever develop. Knowing how to effectively communicate needs and wants can play a major role in how successful a child will be in preschool, elementary school, and secondary school. Some children arrive at preschool with excellent verbal skills, while others struggle to speak in complete coherent sentences.

When the primary language being spoken in the school and surrounding community is not the primary language of a child's parent, this may contribute to arrested verbal development for some children. Research psychologists Rocio García-Carrión and Lourdes Villardón-Gallego (2016) discuss the phenomenon of verbal skills inequalities in their research on early childhood verbal interaction and warn that, if not detected and corrected early, verbal inequality may be irreversible for some children.

If you want to teach a child how to talk, you have to talk to them. Failure to communicate verbally with a child can result in slow speech development and other learning impairments. There are, of course, some parents and guardians who are nonverbal due to a variety of reasons, and in such situations verbal communication for the children will have to come from other resources. Parents in these situations can consult the family pediatrician or other appropriate professionals for advice suited to their unique family circumstance.

Once a child understands the dynamics of education, they will begin to gather information by asking questions. Very young children can be exhausting in their inquiries, and though it may not seem so at the time, that is actually a good thing. Whether corporeal or intellectual, there is some need implicit in all questions. To paraphrase an old saying derived from the Greek philosopher Plato, necessity is the mother of inquiry.

Even when we know the answers to our questions, we seek to know how much the recipients of our questions know. In the case of children, however, questions are almost always going to be asked in order to gain new knowledge. Despite the arduous task of answering a child's questions, asking questions is a very good habit for children to develop. Simply put, if questions result in knowledge and ignorance is a lack of knowledge, then asking questions reveals one's hunger for knowledge rather than a proclivity for ignorance.

NURTURING EMOTIONS

Questions mature as a child matures and eventually the questions evolve to be more ontological in nature, and more metaphysical, such as "Who am I?" or "Why am I?" At the core of our self-awareness are our emotions, and children learn very early that emotional outbursts are very effective ways to communicate. For example, crying can result in a hug, a feeding, or a clean diaper. Also, smiling or laughing can result in receiving more of whatever caused the joy in the first place. Nurturing a child's emotions requires careful attention to detail because some children have difficulty learning to control their emotions.

Learning how to control their emotions can help children avoid some serious problems when they are older; however, it is more of a learned ability than an instinct. Like most things, self-control is learned by observing others or by trial-and-error experience. Learning self-mastery requires deliberate effort by a child's parent or guardian. It should be mentioned that some parents have children with chemical imbalances that result in behavioral manifestations that require special medical attention, so the assumptions about self-mastery in this section might not be relevant for families in those unique situations.

It is an unavoidable fact that children watch their parents to determine what they perceive to be acceptable behavior, but lacking the maturity to comprehend context, children can misinterpret a parent's behavior. For example, a parent might joke with other adults about sticking their hand into a fire, and the other adults present implicitly understand that "I am just joking, and would never really put my hand into a fire." Young children might fail to see the absurdity and facetiousness of the joke.

Parents should be mindful that their children only observe them doing things that are rational within and outside of the context of any given situation, such as working hard, being honest, controlling anger, or being friendly to others. There is nothing wrong with joking, but it might be more productive (perhaps safer, too) for parents to teach children how to discern between joviality and solemnity.

NURTURING THE INTELLECT

Children will have years of formal education from preschool through high school, and even beyond for those who attend trade schools or college. The amount of success children experience during their years of formal education will be largely based on the amount of intellectual nurturing they receive in the home before and during those formative educational years. The most basic and effective way to nurture a young child's intellect is to read to them. The ability to read and comprehend literature is the key to all other knowledge because it unlocks doors that would otherwise remain intellectually closed, including the doors to math, science, and technology.

In addition to the acquisition of knowledge from information contained in books read to them, children also experience self-discovery when they learn how to read for themselves. As they discover which literary genres they prefer, a child's personality develops and matures. Learning to read can also increase their self-confidence. Of course some genres are more intellectually stimulating than others, and for that reason parents should be mindful of which genres their children are reading in order to give them a healthy literary balance.

Music is also an excellent way to provide intellectual nurturing to children, and the earlier the better because the benefits of music on high academic achievement is well-documented. Learning to read music and play a musical instrument incorporates both reading and mathematics, and many researchers believe that is why music has a real measurable effect on academic achievement.

The discipline involved in playing a musical instrument can also help children to learn self-control. It is interesting to compare the students of any school who are exceptional in citizenship, academics, and music because, more times than not, they are the same individuals. Beyond just passively listening to music, it is far more effective to be actively engaged in learning to play a musical instrument. The successful musician learns very quickly that their best results are achieved when they sacrifice time in other endeavors to master their instrument.

A willingness to sacrifice time in order to perfect musical talent is also an excellent characteristic for learning self-control, which comes from patience and the acceptance of delayed gratification. Any student who has endured the torturous regimen of learning to play a musical instrument understands the benefits of self-discipline once they have mastered their instrument. When cost is a factor, parents should inquire as to any special programs for purchasing or renting musical instruments. Hungry for Music (https://hungryformusic.org/instruments/request-an-instrument/) and organizations like it can be good resources for the budget-strapped family.

NURTURING SELF-AWARENESS AND POTENTIAL

There is a myth that we only use 10 percent of our brain capacity, but that is only a myth. We do, however, seldom reach our greatest intellectual potential. How a child learns and uses knowledge they acquire will affect their intellectual potential.

Beyond just learning, however, a child needs to become more aware of his or her own strengths and weaknesses. Understanding strengths and weaknesses is a progression in self-awareness, beyond just being aware of our basic senses. Once a child becomes self-aware by understanding strengths and weaknesses, they can begin to explore their potential.

Most children are good at several things, but typically they are only exceptional at a few things, or, in most cases, just one thing. Discovering the latter is vital to realizing true potential. Physical or intellectual competition is one way to discover strengths and weaknesses, and, incidentally, is an excellent way to learn how to turn weaknesses into strengths. The latter is an important component for a child learning their true potential, but unfortunately some children will give up some pursuits after a few failures. If we learn anything from successful people, it is that an apparent weakness can become a strength.

When allowed to do so, children naturally gravitate to the type of competition they enjoy, such as sports, writing, spelling, music, science, and art, to name a few. Introducing children to competition also introduces them to one of life's inescapable veracities, *opposition*. With opposition comes *adversity*, and in addition to adversity, healthy competition introduces children to *diversity*. It is also helpful to teach children that opposition is natural and does not have to precipitate contention. Healthy competition teaches children how to work as part of a team and how to successfully collaborate with others.

Participation in some sports has traditionally been cost prohibitive to lower-income families, but that has changed significantly in recent years.

Sports that were once only readily available to the affluent have become more and more accessible to all who wish to participate. The desire to be exclusive has been replaced with the desire to win, and as a result, some amateur sports organizations have fee sponsorship and scholarship programs to help them attract and recruit young talent in lower-income communities. Parents should use caution and do their research before allowing their children to join any sports programs.

Another limiting factor for some children who want to compete in amateur athletics is a perceived disability. The word *perceived* is used because in many cases the child does not see themselves as disabled. We only need to look at the amazing athletes who participate in the International Paralympic Committee's Summer and Winter Games to see that the latter is true. Any athlete, regardless of physical appearance, who competes at the world level is the best at what he or she does.

For some children it will be extremely difficult to overcome the innate fear of failure that exists in so many humans, but this can hamper their ability to achieve at their full potential when older. Helping children to overcome their fear of failure and to understand that weaknesses can become strengths will help build confidence. Developmental psychologist Marilyn Price-Mitchell (2013) believes that *resilience* is the result of a child's ability to persevere in the face of failure.

CONCLUSION

There are many aspects to nurturing, and they are all critical to the fundamental development of children. Parents and guardians should adapt the practices for the emotional, physical, and intellectual development of their children. There is no one-size-fits-all solution for nurturing children, so it will take research and trial and error. For the latter reason, it is imperative to reach out to subject-matter experts and also to other parents.

Parents should provide every opportunity for their child to succeed, and a very good place to start is by paying very close attention to how their child is developing through the various phases of their young life. Parents should be aware of what works best for the nurturing of *their* child, as opposed to what proponents of a particular system or technique are saying. Every child is different and develops and grows emotionally and intellectually at their own unique rate. Many parents with two or more children learn quickly that children come equipped with their own unique, innate mannerisms, and what was typical of one is not necessarily typical for the other.

KEY IDEAS TO REMEMBER

- Despite the arduous task of answering a child's questions, asking questions is a very good habit for children to develop.
- Learning how to control emotions could help children avoid serious problems when older.
- Willingness to sacrifice time in order to perfect musical talent is an excellent characteristic for learning self-control.
- Understanding strengths and weaknesses is a progression in self-awareness.
- Helping children to overcome fear of failure can help them to build self-confidence.

Chapter Two

Life Lessons Learned
Within the Family

It remains an indisputable fact that some of the most important teaching is that which goes on within the walls of our own homes. David O. McKay, a schoolteacher and respected member of his community and respected leader of his church, said, "Nothing can take the place of home in rearing and teaching children, and no other success can compensate for failure in the home" (1968). It is in the home and within the family dynamic where children learn how to adhere to and function in structured environments. Learning about home rules, why they exist, and how they work will prepare children for the rules they will face later in life.

RULES—WHY WE HAVE THEM AND WHY WE FOLLOW THEM

Laws are just another form of rules, but breaking them often results in much harsher punishments than breaking a rule set by parents in a home. Teaching children the importance of following rules can help them to develop a law-abiding attitude when they are older. It is also important to teach children how rules are often meant to protect them and assure equity for access to opportunities.

With regard to protection, if there is, for example, an established rule that no one is to go swimming in the family pool alone, then the chance of accidental drowning is greatly reduced. The latter concept might be difficult for very young children to understand, but parents could try emphasizing that they will be *safer* if they follow that rule. Children learn the meaning of the word *safe* relatively early in childhood, and therefore often develop positive associations with anything that they perceive as safe.

Rules can assure equity when there is too little of something and too many interested parties; in this case, the *interested parties* are children or other family members. The only way to assure that everyone has an opportunity to enjoy the limited resource is to establish a set of rules based on sharing. For example, if there is one piano and several members of the family want to play that piano, parents might establish a time schedule that outlines when each interested family member is scheduled to play the piano.

As with the example of the piano, some opportunities exist only because there are rules (or laws) that exist to assure equal access. The excess or absence of access has been at the center of political debates for decades, but at some level, anyone who has enjoyed access to something that is otherwise limited owes their good fortune to a rule or policy that made it possible. Entire systems of government are based on the latter truth.

FOCUS ON THE *DOS* BUT UNDERSTAND THE *DON'TS*

There is no avoiding the fact that most rules include *don'ts* as well as *dos*, but how one looks at these two components of rules could determine how well they learn to work in structured environments. An old axiom goes "Rules were made to be broken," but that is not a very accurate or productive way of looking at rules. Certainly, breaking rules as a custom could ultimately limit a person's success or achievement because it could lead to mistrust, which could lead to the loss of access to life-promoting opportunities.

Losing trust and access to opportunities will most commonly result in failure, and that is the opposite of what every good parent wants for their children. Therefore, it is best to teach children that rules should be followed. It is true that not all rules are fair or equitable, but there are ways to challenge rules or to avoid the situations that make the rules applicable. Whatever the case, children should be taught what the rules are, within the home or wherever, and why they exist.

One approach is to teach children how to focus on the *dos* of rules, and what they are allowed to do within the rules. Using the example again of a rule for the family pool can demonstrate that the rule actually implies that everyone has the right to swim in the family pool. In other words, no one person is allowed to selfishly have the pool all to themselves. Also implicit in a rule *that no one swims alone* is that swimming is an opportunity to communicate with and spend time with other family members.

Recognizing the privileges available within a set of rules will help children to avoid a perception of restriction later in life when subjected to rules they must adhere to outside of the home. Learning to see the *glass-half-full* side of rules can be a healthy exercise for building self-confidence and avoiding the victim trap.

It would be insincere to imply that all rules are optimistic for everyone. The truth is that sometimes rules are exclusive and not equitable for everyone. Incidentally, there have been and still are laws that result in limited or no access for some and unlimited access for others. While it might lead some to conclude that such laws are wrong, that is not always the case. The selectivity could be intended to protect those who are excluded. For example, some amusement park ride rules deliberately discriminate based on physical attributes, but those are meant to keep riders safe.

Whatever the perception of a rule, more times than not, obeying the rule will result in a positive outcome. Also, most have the option to avoid institutions and organizations where exclusive rules exist; loss of business or negative public relations is quite often the most effective way to change exclusive rules.

FAMILY RELATIONS

Within the family there is a hierarchy of authority and leadership, with the parents at the highest level. Children are typically placed within the hierarchy by age, where the youngest member of the family has the least amount of authority. There are several factors that establish family hierarchical assignments, and here we focus on three:

Trustworthiness
Physical Dominance
Intellectual Dominance

While physical dominance or intellectual dominance are definitely legitimate traits to have in order to have a lofty assignment in the family hierarchy dynamic, trustworthiness is probably the most effective of the three.

Being a member of the family does not guarantee that you will be considered by family members to be trustworthy. Parents and children must earn the trust of family members, and their history within the family determines if they are perceived as trustworthy. Age also determines how quickly trust-worthiness is earned. For example, a parent will be held to a higher standard of trustworthiness than a child because children assume that parents are honest. When parents violate that perception of honesty, it is very difficult to regain that trust, but it is not impossible. It is best to always be honest because children are always watching.

One act of kindness followed by another is how trust is earned. Like building a house, constructing a relationship of trust requires planning, patience, and more than minimal effort. It is easier for a parent to establish trust when their children are young because children rely on parents for every basic need. If a parent is attentive to providing those basic needs, then children will respond with unconditional trust pertaining to that component of the parent-child relationship.

Trust hierarchy goes from the parent down, and in some families the oldest sibling has a level of trust equal to the parents in the eyes of their younger siblings. The older siblings learn trustworthiness by watching the examples of the parents. The younger siblings' perceptions of older sibling trustworthiness are based on how well the older siblings match perceptions of parent trustworthiness.

Another factor in the role of family hierarchy is *physical dominance* or at least the perception of it. While some children will grow up to be taller and more physically imposing than their parents, in most cases the respect established when the children are younger will persist. The 1977 documentary *Pumping Iron* which featured—among others—bodybuilding goliaths Arnold Schwarzenegger and Lou Ferrigno, captured the hearts of its audience with the relationship of Lou Ferrigno and his father.

Although Lou Ferrigno's father was several inches shorter and weighed at least a hundred pounds less than the bodybuilding legend, the respect that Lou Ferrigno had for his father was undeniable. Most parents will not raise a hulk, but there will come a time when their little children are not so little anymore, and respect is not so easily given.

Within the family unit—among other things—physical dominance establishes respect, but lasting respect is developed by showing genuine respect to the other members of the family. Returning to the example of Lou Ferrigno, it is clear that the bodybuilder was not physically intimidated by his father, but he respected him as an authority figure. It is apparent that Lou Ferrigno's father had established himself as a source of reliable advice and counsel while his son was still a child.

Along with physical dominance, parents are usually established as the intellectual superiors of the family when their children are young. Naturally parents know more than their children when their children are very young, but some parents raise intellectual prodigies. For example, Albert Einstein's father was an accomplished engineer in his own right, but he never attained the intellectual stature of his son.

Most parents will not raise an Einstein, but it is not unusual for children to surpass their parents intellectually. With technology, for example, sometimes the roles of parent and child are reversed, and parents find themselves dependent upon the knowledge of the child in order to understand new technology.

Even in cases like the latter, however, children still assume their parents possess knowledge superior to their own. In other words, the intellectual hierarchy remains intact, and parents learn to respect the intellect of their children as a reliable source of knowledge.

There is no other place where the proverbial *golden rule* applies more than within the family. Children learn to treat others based on how they perceive themselves to be treated within the family unit. Children learn to trust others, acknowledge authority, respect hierarchy, and acknowledge the intellectual accomplishments of others based on experiences within the walls of their own homes.

CONCLUSION

There have always been those who feel marginalized and even persecuted by rules and laws, and in more than a few circumstances those feelings have been justified. We only need to go through the annals of world history to confirm the latter statement. It is, however, important that parents teach their children how to discern between the good rules and the bad rules. Also, it is crucial for parents to teach their children that they can always choose not to utilize the resources of groups, organizations, or other entities that have rules that discriminate against them or others without just cause.

Family dynamics is the best place for children to learn about human relations and to develop their human interaction skills. Technology enables people to communicate instantaneously while they are physically remote from each other, but while this phenomenon is great for rapid communication and the rapid distribution of information, it is not necessarily healthy for the development of social skills. In order to learn about human interaction and perfect your skills at it, you must interact with real people. There is no substitute.

KEY IDEAS TO REMEMBER

- It is important to teach children how rules are often meant to protect them and to assure equity with regard to opportunities.
- Teach children how to focus on the *do*s of rules rather than the *don't*s.
- One act of kindness followed by another is how trust is earned.
- There is no other place where the proverbial *golden rule* applies more than within the family.

Chapter Three

Family History

Volumes of scientific, philosophical, and theological research and doctrine are dedicated to the questions "Who am I?" and "Where did I come from?"; however, for the purpose of this chapter, the answer to those existential questions will not be as incomprehensible as some scientists, philosophers, and theologians make them out to be. It is maintained here—simplistically and nonmetaphysically—that we come from our ancestors, and we are the by-products of their genetic substances.

At the very least we owe our genetic traits and characteristics to our ancestors, but our debts to those who came before are more than eye color and hair color. Some of our ancestors made great sacrifices to assure a better life for us, their descendants. One way to honor our ancestors is to find out who they were and how they lived.

ANCESTORS—WHAT CAN YOU LEARN FROM THEM?

For every biography or autobiography of a famous historical figure, there are volumes of untold histories of common people. The histories of lesser-known people are untold because of a lack of historical significance to their societies as a whole, but their histories should be important to their progenies. Since the ancestors of most people do not have historical implications, it is up to posterity to search out the histories of ancestral family members, and then preserve them.

It used to be that only professionals like academic scholars, anthropologists, or professional genealogists could competently research the origins of a family, but with the rapid growth of computer technology and advances made to the Internet, it has become possible for anyone (who has the desire) to become a competent family history researcher.

Within the last decade there has been an upsurge of websites that offer databases filled with census records, marriage records, death records, military service records, and property records. All of these websites and their extensive databases exist for the sole purpose of assisting professional genealogists and amateur family history researchers.

Some of the most popular of the family history and genealogy websites are Ancestry, RootsWeb, and FamilySearch. The National Archives and other government-sponsored websites are also excellent resources; however, getting started can be a daunting process if you are not sure of what to do. There are professional genealogists who can assist you with getting started with your family history research, and they are no farther than an Internet search away.

The Church of Jesus Christ of Latter-day Saints (aka the LDS Church or the Mormon Church) have Family History Centers located throughout the United States and other parts of the world, and they offer free family history research services to professional and amateur genealogists. The nearest LDS Family History Center to you can be located by visiting the FamilySearch website at https://www.familysearch.org/locations/ and typing the name of your city and state (or city and country) into the search window.

According to most family history consultants and genealogists, it is most productive to gather as much information about your family as you can before seeking assistance from the experts. Gathering the names, birthdates, birthplaces, marriage dates, marriage places, death dates, and even old school yearbooks of deceased family members will provide you and the person assisting you with a wealth of information to use for initiating your family history research.

If you are confident enough to venture out on your own and just use Internet resources, then having a good cache of information can help speed along the research process when using online programs. There are resources such as family group sheet templates or family pedigree chart templates available on most of the genealogical and family history websites. Everything you will need to get started is right at your fingertips, and all you have to supply is motivation and sincere desire.

CULTURE—WHO YOU ARE AND WHY THAT MATTERS

According to the online Merriam-Webster dictionary definition for *culture*, it is "the beliefs, customs, arts, etc., of a particular society, group, place, or time" (2016). History has shown that it is the diversity of cultures within a society that perpetuates its growth, and that is true for just about anything from language and art to science and technology. The growth of the communities in which we live depends on our cultural sharing.

Children are first introduced to culture by immediate family members, including parents, siblings, and other relatives. In some cases, neighborhoods are composed of individuals and families who belong to community subcultures that are unique to the macro-culture of the cities or nations in which they live. Some children are ashamed of the uniqueness of their family or community subcultures, and hide their cultural identities. Sometimes shame of culture is the result of bigotry due to political or historical stigmas associated with a culture.

Just as a society averse to intercultural assimilation would stagnate its economic and technological growth, individuals opposed to cultural sharing may stagnate their intellectual and social growth. It is beneficial for children to learn how to absorb knowledge from other cultures, and it is also beneficial for children to share their culture. Before a child can share their culture, they must first know and understand it.

In order to know and understand their culture, children must be taught which traditions or customs comprise their culture. As discussed in the previous section on ancestors, a good place to start is by teaching children their family history. It is also important to teach children about the villains as well as the heroes or the bitter nuts as well as the sweet fruit on the family tree.

FAMILY TRADITIONS—MAKE GOOD ONES AND PRESERVE THEM

Any consistent event or activity that is repeated on or around a certain date by family members can be a family tradition. Some family traditions are annual, like getting together for holidays, birthdays, or summer vacations. Some family traditions are weekly, like going to see a movie, water-skiing, or getting together for a Sunday afternoon dinner. Family traditions need not be complex or elaborate but could be as simple as getting together and going for a walk around the neighborhood park or forming a family book club and reading books together. The most important family tradition ingredient is just getting together.

While it is a simple phrase, *getting together* can be very challenging. Vast numbers of technological advancements have made life easier and more efficient in many ways, but they have also made life more complex and less efficient in other ways. For example, cable TV, satellite TV, and internet streaming have made it possible to watch almost any TV program from any part of the world at any time of day, but in many cases the surfeit of television program content causes family members to view television alone due to tastes and preferences.

It has been said that we should not sacrifice what we want most for what we want now. Implicit in that statement is that sometimes we might have to sacrifice what we want now in order to keep what we want most. If parents want long-lasting relationships with their children built on trust, loyalty, integrity, and love, then parents should be willing to sacrifice the minor things that prevent family time together. Of course, there are some obstacles to family time that cannot be sacrificed, such as careers or education, but most other things can be put off once a week or once a month to allow families to get together and form family traditions.

If parents start good traditions or carry on the good traditions of the families from which they come, then their children will be more likely to keep and start good traditions when they are grown and have families of their own. A very well-worn phrase that deserves the repetitive use it gets is "A family that plays together, stays together." Now here is where it might be pertinent to clarify any perceptions of naiveté in the preceding statements concerning family traditions and getting together.

For some people, *family* means one parent and one child, or *family* could mean a foster home with foster parents and brothers and sisters who are not biologically related. In the case of a single parent, getting together might be hampered by the reality of having to work long hours while the children are in school or at daycare, and evenings consist of the parent getting the children to bed so that the parent can get to bed in time to get a minimal amount of sleep before starting their day all over again. Foster family get-togethers may be complicated by the dynamics of foster children coming and going or by restrictions imposed by foster care agencies.

The overworked, time-limited, single parent might create traditions by developing a simple ritual that does not require a lot of time or even physically getting together. For example, a single parent could start a tradition of leaving little love notes for their children in secret places every day or some other daily ritual that the children come to expect. Incidentally, love notes could also be a great substitute for presents on special occasions.

Developing traditions in foster families and families with shared custody of children will take a little more creative effort, but it can be done. If foster parents have access to biological parents or relatives, then they might consider finding out something unique (preferably something positive or optimistic) about the families of the foster child, and use that information to pass on a tradition or develop a new tradition. Some of the traditions of one foster child's biological family could become a tradition for other foster children in the home.

Families with shared custody situations where the children live part-time in two different homes could work together to maintain traditions, or one home could create a new tradition and the other home could maintain an old tradition or also create a new tradition. One thing that is not productive in situations of shared custody is for both homes to create an atmosphere of contentious competition against one another; so, though it might be difficult, it is more productive for children to see their divorced parents as allies (Chirban, 2016).

CONCLUSION

It seems that much too often families allow the minor things to supersede the major things. To paraphrase a fairly common workplace statement:

> When you are on your deathbed, you will probably not be thinking about how you wish you had more time on that last project at work, but you will be thinking of how you wish you had more time with the ones you love.

The tragedy of that statement is that all too often people realize that they did not spend their time doing what mattered most.

It was not the purpose of this chapter to minimize or trivialize the importance of work and career; its purpose was to provide a guide for how to solidify family relations through family history, by learning about and sharing family culture, and by keeping or creating family traditions. Eventually the family traditions become legacies carried on by subsequent generations.

KEY IDEAS TO REMEMBER

- One way to honor our ancestors is to find out who they were and how they lived.
- There are dozens of online databases for genealogy research, and some of the most popular are Ancestry, RootsWeb, and FamilySearch.
- It is beneficial for children to learn how to absorb knowledge from other cultures, and it is also beneficial for children to share their culture.
- The most important family tradition ingredient is just getting together.

Chapter Four

Family Legacy

The home is the laboratory of our lives, and what we learn there largely determines what we do when we leave there.

—Thomas S. Monson

There are many things that we inherit from our parents and grandparents. For some of us *inheritance* might include money, real estate, or even valuable heirlooms, but for the majority of us our inheritance is *knowledge* passed down from the previous generation. This knowledge comes in many forms, such as well-guarded cooking recipes, a family story, a family tradition, religious beliefs, or a *family philosophy*.

FAMILY PHILOSOPHY—WHY WE THINK THE WAY WE THINK

While religious beliefs definitely influence how we view the world around us, it is also true that even within a common religion one family will have a slightly different or radically different philosophy of how their religion is meant to govern their lives. There are probably Baptists, Methodists, Catholics, Muslims, Mormons, agnostics, and atheists in most of the major political parties of the United States, and that is likely more often the result of family philosophy than anything else.

Many of the famous philosophers of classic literature were once students of philosophy, and the philosophies that made them famous are usually modified or evolved versions of the philosophies they were taught as students. This is similar to what happens in families as children grow and develop their own philosophies based on their personal experiences and observations outside of the home. For some their personal philosophies are closely related to their parents' philosophies, and for others their philosophies are radically different from the philosophies of their parents.

With all of the different personal beliefs and philosophies, perhaps the most important thing to remember is that as long as it inspires you to personal improvement, respect for others, and respect for the world around you, then it matters little if the philosophy is yours or your parents'. Gordon B. Hinckley, the author of *Standing for Something*, made the following observations:

> Most of us carry in our hearts a desire to assist the poor, to lift the distressed, to give comfort, hope, and help to all who are in trouble and pain. We recognize the need to heal the wounds of society and replace with optimism and faith the pessimism of our times. There is no need for recrimination or criticism against one another. . . . (49)
>
> None of us needs someone who only points out our areas of weakness and the ways in which we have fallen short. We need someone who encourages us to go forward, to try again, to reach a little higher this time. . . . (49)
>
> Civility covers a host of matters in how one human being relates to another with basic human kindness and goodness. Civility requires us to restrain and control ourselves, and at the same time to act with respect towards others. (53)

It is true that for the most part we all agree on what is right and what is wrong with regard to how we treat one another as fellow human beings. The so-called golden rule is a code by which most humans live; treat others as you would like others to treat you. Unfortunately, there are occasions when people will treat others maliciously because they have been treated maliciously by someone else.

Such behavior can lead to a recurring cycle of abuse, and a pessimistic perspective; "misery loves company" or "do unto others as others have done unto you." Although *doing unto others as others have done unto you* could—in fact—cause us to do something nice to someone else because someone was nice to us, it also implies that we are more inclined to withhold our kindness until someone shows us kindness first. It is better to live by the original golden rule, proactively—rather than reactively—doing something kind.

SERVING OTHERS FIRST

One of the best-kept secrets has to be that a sure way to distract yourself from your own troubles is to serve others. There is just something about forgetting yourself for a while and focusing on what you can do for others. Paraphrasing the famous quote from President John F. Kennedy, "Ask not what [others] can do for you—ask what you can do for [others]." Finding opportunities to serve someone else is fairly easy to do. All you need to do is take a moment to think about a talent, skill, or knowledge that you might possess that will bring happiness to another, and then do it.

Of course, it is important to allow the recipient to be willing because we all have different definitions of what will make us happy. You would not want to offend someone by doing something that they dislike; so, unless it is someone with whom you have a good relationship and you are very familiar with what they may or may not like, it is safest to assess the individual's situation before you offer your free-of–charge, no-attachments service. For example, you would not want to offer to paint your neighbor's house unless you know it is something that they have been meaning to do; otherwise, your offer may offend them.

Several years back there was a graduate student who impressed his professor and fellow graduate students so much with his verbal reading skill that the professor finally had to ask, "How did you learn to read so well?" The graduate student shared with his class that he had a friend who had lost his sight and, for reasons unknown, was unable to read using Braille so the graduate student offered to read books to his friend. After years of reading to his friend, the graduate student developed his amazing talent. The latter is just one of many ways that serving others can benefit the giver of the service as well as the recipient.

Serving others by using all of the good knowledge, skills, and talents obtained at home and in school is an excellent legacy to carry on and pass down to the next generation. Parents, guardians, older siblings, other relatives, and family friends should take every opportunity for children to observe them eagerly engaged in an act of unconditional service to family, friends, strangers, and community.

CREATING AND MAINTAINING A POSITIVE IMAGE

It is believed that first and last impressions are what form a person's perception of who we are, and all of the stuff in between is largely dismissed or forgotten in initial or last contacts (Willis & Todorov, 2006; Todorov & Porter, 2014). What is more implicit in the latter claim is that, since we can never tell at what point those around us are observing us for the first time, it is practical to try to present our absolute best self at all times. Invariably there are times when circumstances will find you presenting a less socially acceptable version of yourself, but even those times do not negate or invalidate a sincere effort to present your most acceptable self.

The phrase "_____ made me angry" is a fallacy, regardless of what fills in the blank, because people choose how they react to the external forces that impact them. While a person cannot always control how others treat them, they can control how they react to how they are treated by others. There is nothing that physically compels a person to react violently when another person acts violently upon them. There are circumstances when people have to defend themselves for their very survival—if they are trapped in a war zone or some other crisis, for example, or by virtue of their professions as in the case of soldiers or police officers—but generally these are rare situations.

The concept of *self-control* or *self-mastery*, as discussed in the "Family Nurturing" chapter of this book, applies to controlling our anger by choosing not to become angry. Learning to live by this concept will help children navigate through a host of situations at home, at school, or just at play. Incidentally, controlling anger by choosing not to become angry will also help adults to navigate through a host of situations at home, at work, or wherever else life might take them. Living by the latter principle will also lead to a more positive life outlook over time.

Having a positive attitude is the essence of what helps others to see a positive image in you. As tempting as it is to share our miseries with others, it is more socially acceptable to share our joys. To be sure, there is a real human need to seek—even to crave—the empathy or sympathy of others, but there is always the danger of giving others the impression that their struggles are less than your own. Even when your struggles are more, it is better to avoid acknowledging it. Also, as previously explained in the *serving others first* section, putting the needs of others before our own can be therapeutic.

CONCLUSION

Everyone takes with them a legacy from the family in which they were raised, and whether good or bad, that legacy influences ideologies and beliefs. The good news is that no one has to be stuck with a bad legacy, and like that saying about turning life's lemons into lemonade, even a bad legacy can inspire a good legacy. As for good legacies, they should be cherished and passed on to posterity.

There is definitely too much anger, impatience, and selfishness all around. In fact, these phenomena have given rise to words like *frenemy* that give the saying "Keep your friends close and keep your enemies closer" a whole new meaning. The best approach is to not wait for opportunities or until someone else initiates benevolence but to be proactively kind to others. Taking the opportunity to reach out to others in kindness first could lead to unexpected, reciprocated generosity; however, that should never be the motivation for being kind to someone else.

KEY IDEAS TO REMEMBER

- For the majority of us, our inheritance is *knowledge* passed down from the previous generation.
- It is better to live by the original golden rule proactively—rather than reactively—by doing something kind.
- As long as it inspires you to personal improvement, respect for others, and respect for the world around you, then it matters little if the philosophy is yours or your parents'.
- Having a positive attitude is the essence of what helps others to see a positive image in you.

Chapter Five

Family and the Technology Gap

It seems that for many parents the very mention of *technology* (perhaps even more so *digital technology*) causes an elevation in blood pressure or extreme anxiety. This *technophobia* is nothing new, and it is definitely not unique to the present generation of technically challenged parents or others who fear or avoid technology; the term was first coined during the mid-eighteenth to mid-nineteenth centuries during the Industrial Revolution.

From the dawn of the Industrial Revolution to the present, parents have experienced technological advancements that completely changed the world as they knew it. Here are just a few of the technological and industrial changes that have taken place over the last 120 years:

- Still photography to motion pictures
- Horse and buggy to automobiles
- Hot-air balloons to airplanes
- Telegraph to telephones
- Slide rules to handheld electronic calculators
- Large mainframe computers to personal desktop computers
- Personal desktop computers to notebook computers
- Notebook computers to tablets
- Tablets to smartphones

The list could go on indefinitely because technology changes exponentially each year, and those who avoid it are in danger of becoming professionally and intellectually extinct.

Rosen (2004) summarized the phenomenon of technological relevancy by pointing out how, in business settings, persons born between 1945 and 1964 prefer *process-oriented* face-to-face meetings while persons born between 1965 and 1980 prefer spontaneity and electronic communication. According to Rosen, the phenomenon is due to later generations being born into a more technologically advanced world than the previous generation. The latter means that professionals of the present generation and beyond not only *will* be but *must* be more proficient in digital technology in order to be successful.

How can parents ever hope to keep up with all of these technological advancements, and how healthy is the rapid evolution of technology for children? In a study concerning parental attitudes about computer usage and digital technology for kindergarten students in Croatia, Mikelić Preradović, Lešin, and Šagud (2016) found that the level of the parent's education had very little effect on parental attitudes about perceived negative outcomes for young children who are introduced to digital technology.

College-educated parents as well as parents without college degrees are concerned about the long-term social impacts from exposure to digital technology. Some studies show that the amount of technology a parent is exposed to may negatively impact the emotional, social, and intellectual development of children. In their study on technology interference with co-parenting, McDaniel and Coyne (2016) found that 96 percent of mothers reported that technology interfered with co-parenting. There should be balance between hands-on family time and family time spent using technology.

When most people speak of a generation gap, they are referring to the differences in social practices and attitudes from one generation to the next. For example, when someone from the generation of the 1950s talks about good dance music, they are most likely talking about something completely different from the dance music preferred by the teenage generation of the 1970s. Equally, the teenage generation of the twenty-first century would probably not agree with the teenage generation of the 1970s.

It is not that difficult to introduce one generation to the music of another, and grandparents might learn to appreciate some of the music of their grandchildren. Conversely, when it comes to the *technology gap*, it is much more difficult to bridge across generations because it requires intellectual growth and hands-on experience. Lectures and literature are not the most adequate way to become familiar with new technology, but real hands-on learning is the most effective way to become proficient with technology.

By the very nature of opposites, for any positive there is a negative, and there are definitely many negatives when it comes to computer technology. However, just as with electricity and automobiles, the positives far outweigh the negatives. While it is true that children can become so obsessed with digital technology that they become addicted, it is also true that as children become more acquainted with the operation of computers and how computer software is created they are more likely to be professionally relevant and marketable when they are older. Incidentally, parents can also benefit by becoming more familiar with computer technology.

THE GOOD, BETTER, AND BEST OF TECHNOLOGY AND THE FAMILY

As with any other tool, if used properly the results can be quite satisfying. In an article to her fellow librarians, reference librarian Clara Hendricks (2015), a member of the Children and Technology Committee of the Association for Library Service to Children (ALSC), lists ten ways to help parents navigate technology with their children:

1. Provide parents and children access to various types of technology
2. Provide opportunities for parent-child engagement with technology
3. Leave your personal opinions at the door
4. Build up parenting collection with books on topics related to technology and children
5. Monitor the ongoing dialogue in libraries and beyond about children and technology
6. Treat technological tools and new media like any other library material
7. Encourage parents to allow children to be their teachers
8. Stay connected with local schools and their use of technology
9. Market the library as a media mentor
10. Promote the library as a technological hub

Although the ten suggestions above were originally intended for librarians, several can easily be adapted to the home. The latter is where we make the transition from good to better.

It is good that local libraries provide parent-child access to technology along with the resources that teach parents and children how to efficiently use technology. Most parents will not have in their homes the resources available at the local library that teach how to use digital technology. Parents should take advantage of the free resources offered by their local libraries, and it certainly does not hurt to occasionally get away from the distractions that can exist at home.

Library outings should be the exception as opposed to the rule of parent-child digital interaction because, wherever possible, it is within the home that parents are going to have more control over how and when their children use technology. It is also within the home that there are going to be more *opportunities for parent-child engagement with technology*.

Perhaps the best approach to technology and family is to establish digital technology aptitude as a family requirement where no one—parent or child—is exempt. Suggesting that families adopt a digital technology aptitude is much easier said than done because it requires some parents to get completely outside of their digital technology–free comfort zones. As alluded to earlier, the fear of technology is as profound as the fear of public speaking or the fear of mathematics. However, just as with a fear of public speaking or math, fear of computers and digital technology can be academically, professionally, and socially crippling.

No matter how fearful a parent is of digital technology, the fact is children learn best when the thing being taught is demonstrated. Most parents know that if they want their children to grow up to be trustworthy individuals, then the parents must demonstrate what it means to be *trustworthy*. Similarly, children will increase in technological competence as parents become more technologically competent.

THE COMPUTER-ILLITERATE GENERATIONS

The generation of people born before the mid-1960s is the most computer illiterate of all current generations. This might seem obvious, but the irony is that those same generations were the first to develop computer technology. From the IBM mainframe to the Microsoft operating system to the Apple personal computer, we owe the discovery and development of today's digital technology to individuals who were born before the 1970s.

If parents only hurt themselves by being computer illiterate, then it would not be an important issue. Unfortunately, parent digital illiteracy can affect how digitally literate their children will be because children will be left to learn on their own or from their teachers without any home support. Just as when parents are unable to read and their children develop reading skills more slowly than their peers, children with parents who are unable to use digital technology will develop those skills more slowly than their peers. No worries though, there are solutions and there is help for the digitally illiterate.

The help that is available at public libraries has already been mentioned, but the digitally challenged parent need not even leave the home in order to gain computer and digital technology literacy. The Internet has more resources to help build digital literacy than could be contained in the pages of this book, and it is just a matter of a search engine click away. There are those who still struggle with how to navigate the Internet, and for those individuals the public library might be the best resource. Computer retailers are another resource because some have excellent customer service representation, which includes hands-on computer training.

There are also some public colleges and universities that allow public access to digital technology resources, as well as offering affordable courses in basic computer technology and computer science. It may well be worth the effort for parents and others lacking in digital technological knowledge to seek out those resources. There could even be a willing young computer science major available during a campus library visit.

Those who work with or study computers can be an excellent resource for learning more about digital technology. Those who work with computers are very enthusiastic about their profession and often welcome the opportunity to teach others. When at a computer retail store, do not be afraid to ask the young computer expert questions about computer usage because it might just be one of the best lectures on computer technology you will ever receive. Parents should take advantage of every opportunity to learn about digital technology and to increase their computer skills.

THE COMPUTER-LITERATE GENERATIONS

While the concept of the Internet dates back to as early as 1961, it was not until 1995 when the Federal Networking Council (Internet Society, 2017) coined the term *Internet* that we had what we know today as the Internet. Given the timeline for the creation of the Internet, it would be more accurate to say that those who were born after 1990 are the most digitally literate generation. It is probably a safe assumption that the offspring of the children born in 1990 and later will be exponentially more digitally literate than their parents and grandparents. What does all of this mean for families?

If each generation is exponentially more digitally literate than the previous generation, then parents should be extra vigilant regarding the technology gap because it will only get wider with each generation. To be clear, the technology gap between generations is not as ominous as it may seem—it is, in fact, good for each generation to be more digitally literate than the previous generation. It is the next generation that will push technology forward to its next stage of evolution, so parents do not want their children to become technologically extinct.

CONCLUSION

The evolution of technology has completely changed how K–12 schools and universities approach learning. New phrases and terms such as *blended learning, gamification,* and *e-learning* are becoming more and more common in the classroom, and traditional textbooks are being replaced with tablets and smartphones. Most of the major colleges and universities offer online courses, and there are even some K–12 public schools that are entirely (and only) accessible on the Internet. The old saying "If you can't beat them, then join them" has never been more relevant than it is to digital technology.

KEY IDEAS TO REMEMBER

- Technology changes exponentially each year, and those who avoid it are in danger of becoming professionally and intellectually extinct.
- There should be a balance between hands-on family time and family time spent using technology.
- Parents should take advantage of the free computer resources offered by their local libraries to occasionally get away from the distractions that can exist at home.
- Computer illiteracy can be academically, professionally, and socially crippling.

II

Education

Introduction to Part II: Education

Steve Sonntag, MA

After one's family is well-established and solidified, there is time for one to be much more receptive about the world around them.

When children are young, teach them to become receptive every day to new experiences and to new information. Children are constantly learning about what it means to be human. Thus, parents talking to their children who seemingly do not understand the words may be assured that they most definitely understand the feelings, and this ultimately helps them to learn how to work with and to react to people along with pursuing their own hopes and dreams as they progress in age.

When they are older, in their teens, these can be promising years filled with possibilities, like a baby kangaroo leaving its mother's pouch in order to explore the surrounding environment.

As they grow out of their teen years, children may be able to start fulfilling their career goals by pursuing a college or vocational education. This is the time for them to become fulfilled through even more educational experiences that can ultimately evolve into a career. While taking college or vocational classes may seem like a daily chore, when one considers every day as one day closer to one's dream job, such a perspective can allow a person to become more focused on achieving their goal of graduation from college or vocational school.

If teens are unsure of what their ultimate dream job might be, parents should encourage their young adults to take as many different kinds of classes as possible. In this way, they can decide for themselves which subjects are most appealing.

If they are anxious or feel pressed by those around them to choose a career, parents should encourage their young adults to take their time to decide. As for the pressure they may feel from others, young adults cannot avoid these comments, although they have every right to disregard them and to focus on what they feel will bring them the most happiness after they have explored many kinds of subjects.

As adults, it is time to establish themselves in one way or another in the work world. It is hoped that they will become very inspired to enjoy the work they pursue. When one is "goal-less," one can find oneself attached to jobs that simply pay the bills and provide some extra spending money. While this is important for a working adult, when one is totally involved in and satisfied with one's work, work can become a place of joy and not something necessarily to be dreaded. One fulfills one's purpose and feels that this career will be the most satisfying.

In order to avoid dreading a job and to become inspired, it is best to take a career interest test available online or in a book. A career interest test can prove very valuable, whether one has a career in mind or not, and can help a person to validate a possible career choice or allow them to consider different options that they may have heard about or that they may have only remotely considered previously. Then it is a matter of going to these workplaces to observe the people and their end products, to ask questions, to contemplate these possible careers, and perhaps even to become inspired for life by a particular choice.

Oftentimes when people have dated over a period of time, they become romantically involved and this may lead to a long-term relationship or marriage. Such a relationship can lead to having children or adopting children or both. Indeed, being a family member is definitely an education to behold and to cherish with hopefully more amazing times than disappointments and challenges.

If there is a conscious decision not to be involved in a relationship, this can be everlasting or short-lived based on the people one encounters.

During one's working years, people may need or want to take classes, which should be encouraged because they will be that much more informed about the world around them. If a class is work-related, there can be an opportunity for possible advancement or an increase in salary involved. If it is for the sake of learning something different above and beyond work, this can be a great way to learn something very unique.

As the years progress for people personally and professionally and even if the job is enjoyed, retirement will be the carrot at the end of the stick, if you will. It can be rather enticing to ponder, although it may be rather a struggle to accept after working so much. Thus, retirement planning indeed needs special attention to ensure that a person has enough income from retirement and any other financial resources for that well-deserved time of relaxation, if that is what one wishes to do.

Thinking of one's retirement years as "the second honeymoon" of one's life, education can still be very important since there is more freedom to do what one wants without the restrictions imposed during the working years. After a while, some people want to give back to the professional community so that future generations can learn from their expertise.

A very interesting way to give back during the school years, the working years, and the retirement years is via the United Nations World Food Programme. Their free website (Free Rice at http://www.freerice.com) allows anyone in the world to validate their learning by seeing how well they can answer multiple-choice questions on many subjects. Once a correct answer is given, a certain amount of rice is given by organizations that produce rice to those nations with populations in need.

It is exceedingly important that we all have a purposeful life, no matter how old we are, and it is also exceedingly important that we do our best to be positive and hopeful. Granted, there are life circumstances, such as the loss of a loved one, that can weigh heavily on our hearts. One must always strive to reach toward goals with the best attitude along with being realistic. It is possible that we may need to be motivated by others.

This part of the book deals with education, along with what it means to be human in a very competitive and oftentimes very stressful world. By understanding the complexity of education and the interaction of people, one's life can improve tremendously. It is then that we have the option to become role models for others who also may need professional support, although they need to be willing to be inspired. In a manner of speaking, it is like the movie *Pay It Forward*, in which one deed by one individual can become the inspiration to help others. Thus, education with inspiration can result in some amazing discoveries and changes.

Chapter Six

School Options

In the past, most parents' only option for their children was to have them attend the nearby public schools. It was just naturally expected that their children would learn the basic subjects from kindergarten to the high school level in the same school district, unless families moved to another part of town or to another town or city, thus necessitating a change in schools or districts.

Due to parents having to commute to their employment, they may have requested an interdistrict or an intradistrict transfer so that their children could attend school closer to where they were employed. Such transfers have also been requested because assigned schools had bad or good reputations.

The curriculum and the methods of presenting it have gone through tremendous changes, with many schools using tablets instead of textbooks in order to reduce the costs of textbooks and in order to reduce body fatigue for students. Nevertheless, even with the conversion to tablets, there are many students who get copies of textbooks from their teachers who still have them available, or their parents buy or rent textbooks for them. Some reasons for this are that they like holding them, highlighting them, and also, if they buy them, they may be planning to keep them for possible future reference, either for advanced high school classes or for their college major.

The traditional public school system has undergone many significant changes, with a lot of experimentation as to the format of the school day and the school year. The school day can consist of the standard six to seven classes a day. Such a model of the school day is what many people have been accustomed to throughout the years. It allows them to have a variety of classes and teachers.

From the students' perspective, such a traditional school system can produce a lot of stress, depending upon the quality of the classes being taken. If they take many challenging classes, this can be an overwhelming experience as they have to focus on so many classes. In turn, once students get home, whether they are involved in sports, work after school, or not, they can feel inundated with a lot of work, thus requiring them to stay up very late. For example, many dedicated students will survive on only five hours or less of sleep each school night. They will "crash" during the weekend in order to try to catch up on their sleep.

Such academic demands and lack of sleep can hinder students in terms of their health as well as in their studies. While they may do their very best to stay "on task" each night, they can reach a breaking point physically, emotionally, and academically, which is counterproductive to their fulfillment as humans and as students.

Physically, because the body can only tolerate so much time being alert until the wee hours, this may ultimately result in complete exhaustion. It can be very emotionally draining and overwhelming trying to cope with the ongoing lack of required sleep. The high demands of classes, such as memorizing new information along with many homework assignments, may result in students giving up and breaking down emotionally. And it can affect them academically. Such a demanding schedule of classes and giving up due to being overwhelmed may very well cause their learning and grades to decline, requiring a major change of the classes.

Another format of the school day is the block schedule, which allows students a full year's instruction in one term of approximately five months. This necessitates that there are fewer classes, typically four classes each term. Such a schedule is similar to a college or a university that is on the semester system.

There are benefits to the block schedule. Students focus that much more on fewer classes. When and if teachers have students with discipline issues, they know that their time with them will be short and over by the end of the term. When and if students do not get along well with their teachers, again, their time together is limited. Lastly, students typically complete an additional class each year when compared to the traditional school system that includes the standard six or seven classes.

There are some disadvantages that need to be considered with regard to the block schedule. Unfortunately, students and teachers get sick or have family emergencies, and they should remain at home. The operative word is "should" since they may easily feel obligated or pressured to attend, even when sick. Students will miss their classes. Granted, they could go online or communicate with their classmates in order to determine what the assignments are, although they will not necessarily understand the concepts, unless the classes are easy for them. Upon returning to school, they may need to get their teachers' help before or after class.

When students take Advanced Placement classes during the first term and the Advanced Placement exams for potential college credit are during the second term, independent review and study groups will be advantageous. When students already have a new set of classes, this situation often creates additional stress on them and may even affect their accomplishments in their current set of classes.

Teachers who are sick or out of class for any amount of time will have to develop teacher lesson plans for their substitute teachers, ideally those who know the subject material. On the other hand, if a substitute does not know the subject material, a teacher's lesson plans need to be developed as precisely as possible in order to attempt to ensure that student learning continues in their absence. In such circumstances, students will have to rely on one another, their textbooks, websites, and apps in order to understand challenging subject material to the best of their ability until the teacher's return.

The block schedule can create a tremendous amount of stress, requiring students to try to learn as much information as possible. The curriculum can be very demanding, and it truly does put much more pressure on students to learn the information and to earn the highest possible grade. For students who are very conscientious, that can easily translate into many hours of study and perhaps sleepless nights.

With more majors to choose from due to our expanding economic society on a global scale, more public schools have done their best to diversify. There are special academies within the regular school that allow students to take specialized classes. There are charter schools that include their own majors, such as for culinary arts, teaching, science, technology, engineering, and mathematics, while students still learn the other basic subjects at the same time.

As a result of such specializations, parents have many more options to choose from. There are parents who select homes in specific areas of their town or city on account of what is being offered and where. Others make arrangements to have their children brought to and picked up from these specialized schools with the permission of these school districts. Also, this allows working parents to have access to their children in the event there are emergencies of any kind, although this is possible no matter where they attend school.

With such popularity, there have been instances of waiting lists, requiring students to wait for another student to graduate or to drop out, for example. If the waiting students can be placed in these specialized schools, fine. If not, students need to wait, or else they simply need to pursue other options for schooling.

Students are apt to feel more receptive to learning when the curriculum that is being offered is to their liking. They will tend to earn higher grades. As a result, these inspired students will be more focused and are more apt to create fewer discipline problems. There may be a more realistic chance that they will wish to pursue a career in these professions; at least, they will gain a better appreciation of the field from such a curriculum should they decide to entertain another career option instead.

Children of parents who are extremely religious oftentimes attend such schools where there are fewer student discipline issues with much more emphasis placed on academics and religion. Such religious schools usually do cost a lot of money, although parents either are able to afford such an education or are able to receive reductions in the tuition by means of scholarships. Also, parents may be able to work on specific days in classes or during special events, such as fairs, for example.

If the family has enough income so that one parent can remain at home in order to teach the children, he or she may wish to consider homeschooling. Of course, he or she needs to be a good planner. Also, seeing that homeschool teachers oftentimes teach their own children, they know them very well, thus providing some advantages and disadvantages.

One advantage of homeschooling is that while guided by the local school district's curriculum or by the curriculum on the internet, for example, parents can go at a faster rate of instruction, provided that the children can learn the information more quickly. Another advantage is that field trips can be made to different areas without going through the typical red tape that regular schools require, provided that such trips are pertinent to what is being taught and provided that it is financially feasible.

On the other hand, the parent-child relationship and the teacher-student relationship combination can create disadvantages. When the parent and the child work with one another, if there is a grudge or a bad day for either one of them, it may be challenging to overcome whatever issue prior to the switch of their roles from parent to teacher and child to student.

Having a teacher from outside the home with a specialty of one or more subjects can definitely help out so that there can be more objectivity than subjectivity. This possibility can be especially helpful when a parent does not know the information of a subject.

While the advantage of homeschooling can be that students may learn at a faster rate, the disadvantage is that they may not have the same amount of interaction with other students in their age group, which may translate into them being less capable of knowing how to interact with others of their own age group. On the other hand, there are homeschool organizations that work with other homeschool organizations that have social events for the students.

When the children are of high school age, when they are usually mature enough and intelligent enough to do so, a great experience for them is to take classes online or at local colleges and local universities along with their regular high school classes. In this way, they can advance their knowledge in a specific field for which they may be able to receive high school credit and college credit. Of course, this is something that needs to be discussed with the high school counselor and the college counselor.

Even if college credit is not awarded for these kinds of classes, there are some definite advantages. Students can learn much more about what it is like to pursue a higher level of education. They learn about subjects in more depth. They can meet other students of their own age group along with college-aged students.

If attending as a high school student under the guidelines of a charter school, it is suggested that a student take only one college class instead of several classes, because high school students will soon discover how thoroughly they need to know the material and how long it is going to take to learn the information very well. It will take many hours for each college class in order to possibly do well in such a class.

If the family needs to be overseas for any amount of time, parents probably know about different school options. Perhaps, they can learn the language of the foreign country as well, if it is not their mother tongue. These families can learn about different cultures, different foods, and simply enjoy being away from the environment that they have been so accustomed to for all of their lives so far. For these elementary and high school students, it is best to check for classes at schools of the mother tongue and/or to go online in order to research for online education.

Online education is a great option for students wanting to advance their studies, or when this is the only option available based upon where they live or due to their circumstances such as long-term illnesses. As for advancing their studies online, this is definitely a possibility when desired subjects are not available at the schools they normally attend. If they wish to earn credit towards graduation, then talking with the counselor or the administration needs to be pursued.

In terms of college- or university-level experiences, when and if it is financially feasible and when and if the high school students' families are willing, it is a great experience for high school students to study overseas for a semester or for a school year. It is especially important that they be very mature in order to consider such a program. After all, it is a major adjustment for a high school student and for the rest of the family to be apart for a long time such as this; however, such an experience can be that much more maturing and very educational.

There is a very interesting program designed for college students that allows them to study on board a ship along with stopping at different ports of call to visit the local attractions and to experience the environment of different countries. This is called Semester at Sea (https://www.semesteratsea.org). If interested, please go to their website.

Education has undergone some major, dynamic changes with most of these changes benefiting the students themselves. Selecting the best option based upon where one lives is extremely important. It is suggested that families discuss the options available so that the students' educational goals are considered. After all, the students' current and future education is reliant upon important planning.

If students have not decided on specific careers, it is best for them to attend schools with the most variety of classes so that they are able to determine what they may wish to do in the future as their career.

KEY IDEAS TO REMEMBER

- The traditional school system has undergone many changes.
- The block schedule has its advantages and its challenges.

- Religious families can benefit by having their children attend religious schools.
- Homeschooling provides individual learning, although it can bring its challenges.
- Online schools can help students who excel without having other students present.
- Studying overseas for a semester or for a year can provide a great opportunity for high school–aged children.

Chapter Seven

Mutual Respect

In life, it is hoped that there is mutual respect in which there is equality in terms of treatment by everybody, thus hopefully creating more harmony and more happiness. The very basis for mutual respect is that open discussion and listening are exercised consistently and genuinely. When people know that they can tactfully and respectfully express their opinions and concerns with one another without any possibility of being judged or degraded, this provides them an opportunity for a very positive relationship, even with differing viewpoints. When people are being heard, trust can become the outcome.

Nevertheless, this is unfortunately not widely practiced. A very good example is the Stanford prison experiment that took place in 1971 in which a team of researchers led by a psychology professor asked for college student volunteers to take on the roles of guards and prisoners. The end result was that those who played the roles of the guards became vindictive toward and abusive of those who played the roles of the prisoners. Those who played the roles of the prisoners became both fearful and resentful of their undeserved treatment.

In that experiment, the outcomes were dire. The abuse of power by the guards was extreme. There were those who had gained so much authority that they realized how much anger and "need for control" they had within them. Respect for authority was degraded and feared. Self-respect was deflated.

While the Stanford prison experiment is an extreme example, such behaviors unfortunately do exist in history and in our daily lives.

Hitler is the prime, horrid example in which he used his power to dictate the will of the German people. In turn, he incited the extermination of millions of people due to his warped sense of reality.

There are some police officers who have allowed the power of their positions to "get to their heads," although police departments are learning how to communicate better and thus to work better with the communities that they are serving and protecting. After all, there has been too much violence, and towns and cities wish to circumvent such violence with the ultimate purpose of having harmony and trust by everyone in the communities.

While most bosses treat their employees with respect, allowing them to do the jobs for which they are being paid for the sake of the business, there are some bosses who can be rather domineering and abusive of the power they have gained. They can easily become unreasonable with their requests.

Some male bosses use their power of authority over female employees to be very demanding for their own personal pleasure, or these male bosses persuade their employees to work many more hours above and beyond their normal hours. Some employees have suffered harassment from their male bosses who know their employees need their jobs and the money. There are some female bosses who have used their authority over both sexes in order to feel powerful and vindictive as well.

Granted, there are ways for employees to counter such negative practices by their bosses, although it truly does take a lot of courage to do so. They may wish to hire attorneys in order to support their cause. There are support groups, such as unions, that can help alleviate any misuse of power. Otherwise, these employees may just wish to quit their jobs in order to prevent themselves from enduring any more stress and harassment than they already have experienced, if it is economically feasible or if they have found another job.

In the teaching world, teachers typically have the knowledge and many years of experience. While most teachers do believe that respect needs to be earned, some of them almost demand respect. They seem to feel entitled to demand it because they are in authority. They may give lengthy lectures with a limited amount of questions permitted. There is little or no time for student discussions to explore the subjects together. Teachers may give extensive assignments both during the week and over the weekend. They also can be very strict in their grading methods.

I have encountered some students whose teachers are the only ones who teach specific courses, and these students have no other choice but to take these courses. Students and their parents have oftentimes complained about how irritating and insensitive some teachers can be, asserting that they do not realize that they are the paid "servants" of these students and parents, employed in order to provide students with a well-rounded education. Some do complain to the administration, but they feel that some teachers remain in their jobs due to tenure and, unfortunately, continue being authoritarians.

Before administrators conduct meetings with students, parents, and teachers, they most likely first meet with the teachers in order to get their perspective regarding the situation. In this way, the administrators will have a better understanding of the teachers' viewpoints.

Afterward, it is best for administrators to meet with students, parents, and teachers in order to discuss tactfully, reasonably, and fairly what is going on so that the classroom environment returns to one of mutual respect and the focus on education is resumed.

Looking at it from the perspective of teachers, they can become overwhelmed with work and oftentimes by big classes filled with a variety of students who run the full gamut of academic ability, let alone those students who create problems for themselves and for everyone else in the classroom. Teachers can feel stressed out personally or professionally or both and they may vent their frustrations on their students, causing further difficulties.

Successful teachers remember that their students are human beings, just as they are, and that everyone has good days and bad days. Mistakes are made, no matter how old a person is. Nevertheless, teachers are the adults, the role models, and they need to be as consistent and fair as possible with regard to discipline in the classroom, in their teaching methods, and in evaluating the students they serve.

Please consider this comparison. Teachers are like servers at a café or at a restaurant. They offer the menus or the subject matter that needs to be learned. They do the best they can to complete what needs to be served. It is then hoped that the customers or the students are well supplied with information so that when they leave the café or the restaurant, the classroom, they will be full of knowledge.

It should also be noted that students should have and do deserve to have a private life—their classes and school are not their entire life. They need some free time, they have families, they may have jobs or hobbies. They may be playing sports that require time for practice, for travel, and for the actual games. They may have any number of things to take care of and they also have homework from all of their classes to complete, although most students will allow enough time to devote to it.

When teachers assign work for their students to complete, they need to allot the time to do the appropriate correcting and documenting as well. Thus, teachers need to give realistic, challenging assignments that inspire learning and critical thinking. Although students may not necessarily enjoy doing homework, when assignments are realistic and challenging, they may become more inspired to learn, and they may find that they complete assignments in less time.

Once a certain amount of material has been taught, teachers will typically give graded assignments, like quizzes, tests, projects, and final exams. It is important to evaluate these kinds of graded assignments in a timely fashion so that teachers can determine how effectively their students have learned. The operative words are "in a timely fashion"—it is important to avoid taking many days or weeks to inform students of their grades.

If there is a major delay in the reporting of grades, this can create problems from an educational point of view, especially if the classes are sequential in which current information is based on the previous material that has been evaluated. Granted, teachers have multiple classes and need to evaluate many papers. Nevertheless, if supplemental activities that support previous learning are assigned for students to complete while their teachers are assessing previous assignments, then teachers can inform their students of their grades and proceed with the next set of information to be learned.

Equally important is the manner in which students are informed of their progress. If teachers simply post students' grades online or in class without returning the graded assignments, such a practice can undermine learning. When students are permitted to review their graded assignments, they can understand what they have done correctly and incorrectly as well as ask questions of their teachers, thus facilitating the learning process while providing valuable feedback to their teachers as to what materials their students have mastered and in what areas they may require further instruction.

Many teachers feel overwhelmed with the amount of work involved in writing new quizzes and tests for each of their classes. They may rely on previously made-up tests with some modifications or on the textbook companies' tests. Teachers attempt to safeguard these assignments so that there will not be any possibility that former students will share previously graded assignments with current students.

In order to counteract this possibility, it is suggested that teachers develop two different graded assignments for each chapter or unit. Granted, this does require extra work at the beginning. Perhaps, prior to school starting, teachers can develop extra graded assignments. Then, throughout the years, teachers can make minor and major changes to each of the graded assignments and thus have a variety of them available.

Along with graded assignments, another way to empower students is to allow them to take extra quizzes based on the unit or chapter that they are studying. Such quizzes need to be administered by teachers, with students advising the teacher if and when they would like to take them. Of course, whatever the students earn on these extra quizzes should count as additional grades, whether they are high, average, or below-average grades.

Offering such an option is one way to affirm respect for the students along with the subjects being studied. Teachers empower their students by providing them with opportunities to improve their grades along with all of their regularly assigned work for grades.

Another way that teachers can earn the respect of their students is by having them check online for the accuracy of their grades. If mistakes are made by the teachers in entering grades online, students hopefully will still have the graded work that was returned to them to show the teachers so that the appropriate changes can be made. After all, the students own their own grades, and the teachers are the judges and the messengers of their students' grades.

If teachers need to calculate their grades by themselves without the assistance of a computer program, so be it. Teachers usually are accurate. Students typically have a rough estimate of their grades based on the quality of their own work and the grades they usually earn, so they usually will be satisfied with the results.

Another way for teachers to gain respect from their students is to ask them to regularly record their own grades in the same way the teachers do. Then, at the end of a grading period, it is very important for teachers to ask that their students determine their own grades based on their own records. They both determine the grades separately and once the teachers tell them what their grades are, if they are basically identical, this shows everyone that accuracy is the end result with everyone being satisfied.

If and when students need to discuss a grade with their teachers that they believe was miscalculated, it is to the students' advantage to be tactful and respectful. After all, while the students only have grades for their own classes, teachers have many students in each of their classes and it is quite possible for errors to be made, even if grades are posted online. For example, when grades are posted online, one grade can be easily posted on the line above or below for other students, thus causing miscalculations.

Under such circumstances, students and teachers need to provide documentation. Students need to have all of their graded work handy at the time of this discussion. Teachers need to use their grade book or to check online in order to compare and/or contrast the grades for each of the graded assignments so that everything is totally accurate.

When students do not feel totally comfortable discussing issues with teachers, they may easily divulge to their parents what is going on. Of course, if the parents work, communicating with teachers can be rather challenging. Single parents may feel a lot of pressure already due to having to work one or more jobs, thus limiting their time to deal with their young adults' issues. In such instances, parents may simply state that their young adults have to deal with the issues by themselves and that they do not have enough time due to their work schedule.

Of course, such conclusions can have mixed results. Young adults may become more assertive when they discuss issues with their teachers themselves along with learning more about mutual respect. Otherwise, young adults may wish to discuss the situation with their academic counselor. The last possibility is simply to accept and learn from this situation. It really depends on the self-concept of the young adults themselves.

When students trust that their classroom is a safe place to learn and understand how to question in tactful and respectful ways, the chances are minimized for discipline issues to surface because the students know and feel that they are heard, respected, and treated fairly.

Teachers can trust that their classrooms are safe places to teach. They are then able to make steady progress so that students can learn to the best of their ability; being consistently fair with all of their students will result in students respecting them. In turn, students can learn to be more realistically self-confident along with being accountable for their own efforts.

Such a positive atmosphere enhances the chances for mutual respect and a very enjoyable experience for everyone, even though the students may experience some degree of stress or boredom with regard to the material being learned. Nevertheless, teachers can generate enthusiasm for any subject by being salespeople and perhaps even being humorous about what they are teaching. As a result, the students realize that they need to study and learn the material being presented, and they may be able to enjoy the experience of learning even more.

Expressing one's thoughts in a respectful, logical manner should be the norm for both teachers and students. Creative thinking and critical thinking can be the natural, positive results. Also, a relaxed atmosphere where mutual respect is practiced can lead to those times in which light-hearted jokes can be made, all of which can lessen the stress that students feel. When more emphasis is placed on learning, grades will improve, which can also lessen stress for everyone.

Mutual respect practiced in the educational community can have an everlasting impact when these young adults enter the working world and in their personal lives as adults.

KEY IDEAS TO REMEMBER

- Mutual respect results in more harmony and in more happiness for everyone.
- There have been unfortunate examples in which mutual respect has not been practiced.
- Teachers have a difficult job to complete all of their work, although they need to be keenly aware of and sensitive to the students whom they are serving.
- Students and parents need to always address teachers with mutual respect, especially when there are issues that need to be discussed.

Chapter Eight

Humility and Gratitude

When mutual respect is earned in any kind of environment, people have the beginnings of good working relationships. As a result, humility and gratitude may be created and solidified.

"Humility," as defined at http://www.dictionary.com, is "the quality or condition of being humble; modest opinion or estimate of one's own importance, rank, etc."

If offspring have younger siblings, the end result may be that the younger siblings will learn to be more sensitive to others and understand how to work with others in the classroom setting. They learn how to share, even though they may want to have something very badly for themselves alone.

Of course rivalry can and will take place because, when there are siblings, there is apt to be competition for the parents' attention and love. There can be a natural jealousy taking place. There can be a primal need to have what the other sibling has, although children can learn to become more humble about working with others outside the family environment. Indeed, the older siblings usually need to make more sacrifices than the younger ones.

In contrast to families with multiple offspring, it is quite conceivable that single offspring who become their parents' center of attention may essentially become very spoiled, because they do not have to share with any other sibling. They may feel they are entitled to everything, and they may not necessarily feel humble. Of course, single offspring are still heavily influenced by their parents so, depending upon how the parents are and how they work with their child, that truly can make a difference in terms of how their child's attitude about themselves and others develops, both now and in the future.

No matter what their family standing may be, there are many young adults who believe that they are entitled to everything they ask for without considering that they may need to earn whatever it is they wish. They can become selfish and greedy, only wanting more without really appreciating who gives them whatever they want and what has been gifted to them.

Such a background of not earning or feeling that one deserves to receive whatever they wish from their parents can be easily transferred into the educational community. While a majority of students realize the importance of hard work and thus are accountable for their own actions, there are those who think that they are better than other people or that they are entitled to high grades, that their mere presence means they can have whatever they wish. Of course this is hyperbole, although there are those students who have overinflated egos.

Here are some real situations.

I taught typical students in a high school. One of the more intelligent students moved from another state and believed his education in his previous state was much more demanding and superior than that offered in his current state. He oftentimes would brag that he was much more intelligent than anyone else at his current school.

One day, the class was assigned to memorize a certain set of words for homework. The next day, it was readily apparent that the class had not studied. As a result, I chose to give them a "pop quiz" on that material after reminding them of what they were supposed to have studied although they had chosen not to do so. Of course, there were some complaints that it was unfair, but especially by this one boy.

The next school day, the quizzes were returned, most with failing grades. That one particular student who felt that he was better than everyone else also earned an F. He complained out loud in front of the class that he felt that it was totally unfair to have to take such an unannounced quiz and that he failed, and the other students just laughed at his complaints.

For the rest of that school year, he continuously complained about the unfairness of that one particular "pop quiz" due to his earning an F on it, although he typically had earned As on most of his graded work. Indeed, he learned about the responsibility of completing his assignments on a regular basis and the humility of having failed after having bragged so much.

Another teacher related the following account that happened to him one year.

A new high school student that had earned very high grades transferred from another school. The counselor referred him to the Academic Decathlon coach because it was thought he would be a very good contributor to the team.

When they met, the coach mentioned to the student that he would need to attend meetings either before or after school in order to work with the other team members so that they could all help each other learn, and this student agreed. Nevertheless, he chose not to attend these meetings on a regular basis.

Seeing that he was a senior in high school and that he wished to get letters of recommendation for his future colleges, universities, and scholarships, he asked the Academic Decathlon coach, who responded by saying the letter of recommendation would be a realistic account of the student's achievements, and he accepted this condition. The student was evidently rather conceited and living in denial about the importance of responsibility; he just naturally assumed that the teacher would write an exemplary letter of recommendation.

A week later, the student received the Academic Decathlon coach's letter of recommendation. It stated that this student had a lot of potential, although he had not shown his potential on account of not attending team sessions on a regular basis as requested.

The next day, he returned to the Academic Decathlon coach and slammed the letter of recommendation on the desk, stating that it would not benefit him whatsoever and that his parents were going to sue him for slander. Again, the Academic Decathlon coach stated that he had agreed to write a realistic account of the student's work or lack thereof. Of course, such a threat to be sued is chilling, although in the end, the attorney determined that the letter of recommendation was realistic and true, and no slander suit was filed.

Such an unrealistic perspective by young adults is a form of denial that will hopefully be transformed into humility and maturity, although it truly can be aggravating to the people around them who are much more mature and more realistic about what is actually taking place.

Some students believe that they "got" a certain grade or that they were "given" a certain grade, as if teachers randomly decide these are the grades they want to give their students instead of determining the grades they have earned due to their own hard work or lack thereof. It is a specific accounting of the actual work, and the results determine the actual grades.

Teachers need to indicate to their students how grades will be determined at the beginning of the school year, and where and when to find these grades. The only time that teacher discretion should be applied is when a student's grade hovers between one grade and another. It is then that the teacher needs to consider any number of factors to either increase or decrease the grade.

For example, if a student's grade is between a C+ and a B− at the end of a grading period, the teacher may wish to consider the following. If the student had cooperated very well, that may be taken into consideration. If the student's graded work showed improvement, that may be considered. If the student had completed all of the homework, that may be taken into consideration. For semester grades and if final exams are given, if the student has earned a higher grade than normally earned, the student should earn the higher grade. If the student has earned a lower grade than normally earned, the student should earn the lower grade.

Of course, one can argue that final exams are comprehensive and can create additional stress for students, and this is a legitimate concern. Nevertheless, when the teacher has covered all of the information on the final exam, and perhaps even provided some of the questions on the final exam to students in advance, it is then very likely that the students will feel less stress and probably will earn their normal grades or perhaps even higher grades. As a matter of fact, students typically earn approximately the same grades as they normally do throughout the school year, based on their study habits and based on the quality of their homework.

When students wish to make a major issue of how teachers teach and want to note every single error that is made by the teachers, it can be a very draining, very defensive experience for the teachers. Under these circumstances, it is extremely important for teachers to be as tactful and as respectful as possible, although that may be challenging to do, depending upon the amount of student discontent that is shown.

If and when students complain to their parents, their parents may be rather realistic as to what is going on and may wish to delve into the issue with questions in order to clarify the situation. Then they may try to reason with their young adult in order to help them to understand how the teacher determined the grade.

If the students complain to their parents, this can result in a meeting of the teachers, the students, the parents, and the counselors in which the teachers need to hear the complaints and explain what was done and possibly not done.

With appropriate documentation provided by teachers, students and parents may or may not necessarily like the results, but they will have learned a very valuable lesson as to what needs to be done by the students in order to be more successful in the future. This can be very humbling but a good learning experience for the students and the parents especially.

If it is a question of whether teachers have made mistakes or have shown bias against students, such meetings can be very humbling for the teachers. In such cases, there probably will be subsequent meetings required, specifically with the administration, in order to resolve the situation. There also could easily be a lot of scrutiny afterward by all concerned to ensure that objectivity is practiced in fairness to all of the students and to set aside any personal biases by these teachers.

While humility is about being modest, possibly correcting any errors in judgment, and learning from any situation in need of correction, "gratitude" is defined at http://www.dictionary.com as "the quality or feeling of being thankful." Indeed, whether we are young or old, we have a lot to be grateful for. We are alive. We have family. We have friends.

As for living in a country with many freedoms, there were five teachers who came from Spain to teach in the United States. They were attracted by the fact that they were going to earn 100 percent more than what they had been earning in Spain and that they would be able to explore the United States, seeing that none of them had done so previously.

When they became accustomed to the American educational system, they ultimately realized that they had 100 percent more work as well. They had very limited time for their lunch breaks in contrast to the long lunch breaks they had experienced in Spain. They had less time due to their professional obligations for their personal lives, although they took some trips, including rides in limos and traveling out of state during extended weekends and on vacation breaks.

As a result, four out of these five teachers returned to Spain after a year of teaching in the United States, and the fifth one returned a year later. They were grateful for the more relaxed atmosphere that Spain's educational system and lifestyle provided them.

The reason to address the concept of gratitude is because there are many people who have lost this concept of gratitude. They just take whatever is available and whoever is available for granted, and they hardly appreciate what is customary for them and hardly express their gratitude to others.

When appreciation is not expressed, people can rightfully feel offended. Generous people take the time to extend a nice gesture to others and usually without conditions. Of course, if it is expected that favors will be returned, such nice gestures may consequently be looked upon with skepticism.

Let's take a specific example. A man goes into a restaurant to have a meal. The waitress gives him a menu. After reviewing it, he orders a big, expensive meal. He is served. He eats it. She asks him if he would like to have dessert. He doesn't want anything else. He receives the bill. He pays her. He doesn't leave a tip.

All during this exchange with the waitress at the restaurant, the customer never says "please" or "thank you." He just views her as a person doing her job without ever realizing that she is worthy of respect. In a manner of speaking, this waitress is viewed as a slave to the customer. Such a lack of gratitude by this customer can be considered as being inconsiderate and rightfully so by the waitress. While their roles are different, what is not different is the fact that they both deserve to be acknowledged and respected as human beings.

Along with common decency and expressing gratitude, customers should always be genuinely friendly with their servers. In this way, their servers will feel valued as people along with performing their roles.

There is another way to look at gratitude and the working world. Anyone who is involved with the public for the purpose of acquiring sales knows that half of the "buy in" of products is how people interact with one another while the other half of the "buy in" will be the products themselves. So, when people behave negatively or with disrespect or with a lack of gratitude, this reflects on the company and the products being sold.

Kids typically do not express their gratitude very easily, unless and until the parents encourage them to say "thank you" to the individuals who have given them something or have done something for them.

Saying "the magic words"—"please" and "thank you"—are trained responses typically taught by parents to their offspring who do not necessarily know at first what it means to be in some kind of relationship. It might take some training and time to learn this and to practice this, but it is truly a good idea to be done out of courtesy and out of respect for others.

Teachers could express their gratitude to students and their parents in a very personal way during the first couple of months of school. They might call their students' homes in order to identify who they are, to explain the purpose of the class, to thank the students and the parents for being a part of the educational team, to find out if they have any questions, and to see if the study materials, such as textbooks and assignments, are at home.

The purpose of asking the parents if they have any questions is to keep the lines of communication between the parents and the teachers open. So very often, the school only notifies parents in the event there is an absence or if there are discipline issues. When teachers consider making positive phone calls such as those suggested, parents understand that the teachers care about their students and plan to keep the parents informed on a regular basis.

The benefit of asking about the study materials being in the students' homes is that the teachers can give those students extra points or an additional A (if the study materials are at home) while ensuring that the parents understand that their offspring need to bring their study materials home on a regular basis so that they can study and complete their homework. Even if they have completed their homework, there is always something to review, and it is always a good idea to look ahead at the material that they will be studying, if they have the time to do this.

If and when you decide to make these introductory phone calls, if the parents are not home, it is best to call another time so that you can have direct phone conversations with them.

Emailing or texting these parents is strongly discouraged because education is personal, which means that the more personal interaction you can have with families, the better are the chances for quality communication between you and them. After all, if they do have questions or concerns, this gives them the opportunity to ask you directly. Emailing and texting leave much room for interpretation while conversing allows everyone to communicate with one another clearly and quickly.

It is only natural for parents to feel apprehensive when phone calls from school personnel take place because they are usually negative in nature. In fact, one time, one teacher was so very proud of the accomplishments of one of his students that he decided to call the parents. After he identified himself, the parent asked: "What did he do wrong this time?" After he explained that the young adult had earned the highest grade on a major test, an A, the parent could not even respond.

In turn, such phone calls can result in what can be called the "positive snowball effect," the ability to accentuate the positive for the family. Students will feel that they are being valued as individuals as well as people who are learning to the best of their ability. Parents will have a better perspective of their young adults, or else they will understand that it takes a lot of work to learn the information as well as to earn their grades, although the parents really know this.

Teachers also benefit because they will have a better rapport with the parents and with the students. In fact, the students may actually cooperate that much better in the classroom. This can ultimately result in students learning to the best of their ability.

Unfortunately, there will be times when teachers and the administration need to communicate with students and parents about behavior or grade issues. The ideal way to resolve any issue is to have face-to-face meetings either before school or after school. The operative word is "ideal" since parents oftentimes need to work, and such meetings can hinder their ability to arrive at their workplace on time. Also, parents frequently work out of town and they may not be able to meet before or after school.

If parents are available, it is advisable to have face-to-face meetings in which the parents, the students, the counselor, the teacher, and an administrator are present. In this way, not only will they be able to deal with the issues more easily but they will also be able to see one another. Such meetings are valuable because facial expressions and body language are just as important as what is being expressed and resolved.

If face-to-face meetings cannot take place, it is suggested that communicating directly by means of the phone, Skype, or FaceTime is preferable to emailing and texting. While emailing and texting can explain the situation, there is an inability to have a direct dialog in order to resolve the situation completely at the moment.

When communicating with the parents at home, it is extremely important to have the students involved. It is a good idea to have everyone completely understand the situation. In this way, they can all discuss any questions and follow-up questions that may be asked.

It is hoped that some kind of solution can be made. It is also then hoped that the students involved can learn from the experience and make a conscious choice and a continuous effort to improve in terms of their learning or behavior in the classroom. Indeed, this can be a very humbling experience that probably will not be easily tolerated; however, in the long run, such experiences will eventually be viewed as being learning moments that can be reflected upon later in life.

When teachers need to make so-called negative phone calls, it is then a good idea to thank everyone involved in the conversation for their time and to express hope that the issue will be forthwith resolved.

Another form of gratitude can be expressed through handshakes. While such advice may be impractical in the classroom, a gentle "high five" or a gentle "knuckle fist" can be a great way to acknowledge each other rather quickly while still being just as effective as a handshake. This can show students that their teachers appreciate them as individuals, that students have cooperated very well, and also that students are doing a great job in learning the material.

Teachers are learned individuals doing their best to teach their students in many different ways. Any way that students can recognize their teachers' importance will show them the respect that they have justly earned.

Of course, other students may judge this as "kissing up" to their teachers. Nevertheless, if these grateful students express such positive feelings in emails, texts, or before or after class, this can easily be a good way to overcome any such interpretation by other students.

When students express their gratitude to their teachers for helping them understand concepts and for ultimately having earned high grades, their teachers will feel that their work and time spent on behalf of their students has been worthwhile and appreciated as it deserves to be.

A teacher once received a perpetual calendar at the end of the school year that she still has to this very day. It states the following: "You cared enough to share your time so that I could learn. Thank you!" Most students really do appreciate their teachers' work, whether they wish to express it or not. It may take many years for teens to come to the realization that teachers have truly been their advocates; once they are adults, however, they may contact their former teachers by means of social media or by returning to their alma mater in order to express their gratitude.

One way for teachers and students to easily express their gratitude to one another is by saying that they hope they have a great day, a great week, a great weekend, and a great vacation. In this way, everyone is being respected as an individual instead of being considered only in terms of their roles in the classroom.

When there is humility, there is a better appreciation of one another and an acknowledgment that everyone has strengths and also areas where they need to rely on others. When gratitude is expressed for efforts made by and for each other, this truly improves the relationships between all involved.

Boosting everyone's self-concept fosters the "positive snowball effect" and makes relationships better.

KEY IDEAS TO REMEMBER

- Humility is the "quality or condition of being humble, modest."
- When one is humble, this can result in better relationships.
- Gratitude is the "quality or feeling of being thankful."
- When one is thankful for the people around them, others will sense this.
- By being humble and by being grateful, both teachers and students will have a better, more appreciative relationship, all of which can result in a more positive classroom environment.

Chapter Nine

Sensitive Dynamics for Better Learning

When people practice mutual respect, humility, and gratitude with one another, these are the foundations of a positive environment for everyone involved. It is from that point on that it is important to continue promoting positive emotional habits that validate each individual in the group genuinely.

An important thing for a teacher to emphasize to students is that everyone can learn from their successes and their errors—both are learning tools to use in order to become better in the future.

It needs to be understood that there are some students whose strengths do not necessarily fall into each of the subjects they take. Some subjects may be easy while some may be a struggle. When students make even the slightest amount of improvement in their graded work, this is a tremendous success that needs to be validated by teachers. Encouraging students in this way makes it very possible that future successes will more easily take place. Again, a "positive snowball effect" can take place in this class, in their other classes, and quite possibly in their adult lives.

There are those young adults who consistently earn high grades and are really proud of their accomplishments. They rightfully feel good about their achievements. At the same time, humility in knowing that it may have taken a lot of work to produce such success previously needs to be recognized by the students.

Some students may boast outwardly to others and feel superior to others, but such bragging can easily backfire. Braggarts may eventually find themselves to be by themselves. They may sense other students' inability to relate to them. In turn, the braggarts may or may not be able to redeem themselves as being partners with the other students who are learning the material as well. It is only hoped that they will learn to be more sensitive and to express their pride in their accomplishments in simpler, less offensive ways.

Everyone—whether of low, average, or high ability—has their own strengths and weaknesses. A student who ultimately succeeds after having devoted enough time to recognize their areas of weakness may be able to appreciate and be sensitive to others who deserve to be helped so that they too can achieve.

Along with students being sensitive and helpful to one another, it is also critically important that teachers, teacher assistants, counselors, and administrators promote confidence with responsibility. When promoting confidence genuinely, students will feel heard, reassured, and inspired to learn. When the school personnel also emphasize personal responsibility, students will realize and accept that when they are consistently diligent in their study habits at home along with being well-behaved in their classes, they can rest assured that they will have done their best to learn and are more likely to earn high grades.

Such advice for others is extremely important in so many ways. When high-achieving students help lower-achieving students, there is a sense of community in which there will be better communication and better harmony amongst everyone. There will be fewer discipline issues arising. There will be more learning taking place. Grades will be higher. Schools will have a safe environment, a better appreciation, and a better reputation. Such a positive outlook can easily transfer to students' personal lives and to their professional lives as well.

While students and school employees have very demanding lives, so do parents. Homes that have two parents who work tend to allow their young adults to "go with the punches." If they do well, so be it. If they do not do well, so be it, unless there is a major issue. Single parents also have very demanding schedules. They too may allow their young adults to study and to work on their own, partly in order to teach them to accept responsibility but also because they simply do not have much time to assist their children due to working or trying to find work, taking care of the normal bills, and generally trying to fulfill many roles. Of course these descriptions of parents are generalities. Parents of all kinds want the best for their young adults, although it may be rather challenging for them to take care of many problems that their young adults present.

Parents may overlook their young adults who continuously excel and naturally expect excellence because they know these students usually do exemplary work. Also, parents may become so busy with their own jobs and responsibilities that they neglect to say something positive to their offspring about their academic achievements. In turn, the offspring may become rather disheartened. In actuality, they deserve their parents' recognition on a regular basis because, although it is a different kind of work compared to their parents' work, these students work a lot.

If students become devastated when they earn lower grades than they usually do, wise parents give advice that helps to shift students' frustration to thinking about different ways to improve. Genuine encouragement can have everlasting, positive effects that may help to prevent recurrences of lower grades. It is also advisable for parents to offer suggestions to help their offspring as well as to check with them on a regular basis. While asking them daily how they are doing in school would be rather annoying, parents should consult with their students fairly frequently, perhaps every other day, to make sure that they are on track with their studies.

Sometimes when parents recognize and praise their young adults' achievements, they may respond by saying a class is easy or that it is "nothing"; however, they will appreciate their parents' kindness in recognizing and praising them for their accomplishments, and parents will be forever remembered and cherished, whether offspring wish to admit it openly or not. Following the parents' example, if the offspring intend to get married and have their own children, they may also wish to use this technique.

Along with a verbal acknowledgment by the parents, a reward for their hard work can contribute to the "positive snowball effect," further encouraging students to continue their academic efforts. Of course, some parents can ill-afford to offer their young adults cash or a gift and thus may want to consider alternative rewards—possibilities might include sharing extra time engaged in a favorite activity with family or friends, letting them sleep late, or allowing them to "skip" one of their usual chores. Other parents believe that their young adults have already earned their reward by achieving high grades. In other words, it really depends on the family circumstances and philosophies as to what kind of recognition is best suited for all concerned.

The parents of lower-achieving students may have different attitudes as well. When parents become dismayed, their frustration can easily be placed upon their offspring. Such parents will usually give advice, although along with such advice they may also express minor to complete dissatisfaction.

While understandable, their offspring probably are already aware of their parents' displeasure; they may justifiably feel disheartened and may easily give up even trying. Hopefully, they will interact with classmates who can talk at their own level or seek their teachers' help to inspire them to achieve to the highest level.

Freethinkers with positive attitudes believe that they are better than their circumstances, that they have a right to develop their own futures. Such individuals truly can build a better future by becoming more educated, and they will more than likely be humble and more sensitive to others like themselves, possibly even becoming positive role models. Again, the "positive snowball effect" will be in motion.

It is important for teachers and parents to commend those lower-achieving students who do earn high grades after changing their study habits. They definitely deserve recognition for their efforts, and they will appreciate such acknowledgments, which can also help motivate them to continue striving for more successes.

Much is dependent upon the students' own attitudes. They may decide that one instance of failure does not mean the beginning of the end of their achievements—it just means that they need to understand the information better and that they need to determine what they answered correctly and incorrectly on their graded assignments. They may also want to consider other variables, such as having too much homework in other classes, family circumstances that may have influenced them, if they were tired, if they were sick, and anything else that might have contributed to this digression.

Let's look at some examples in terms of effort and determination and how one's attitude can definitely affect the outcome.

An interesting novel regarding one's perspective of the world is *The Critic* by Baltasar Gracián from Spain. This book deals with an educated but negative Robinson Crusoe–like character who is stranded on an island and meets an innocent, positive, native, Friday-like character. The Crusoe-like character shares with the Friday-like character all of his misgivings about society while on this island. A boat subsequently retrieves these two individuals and brings them to civilization.

The Friday-like character then discovers that, while there are issues about city life as was described by the Crusoe-like character, there are plenty of wonderful things about life to appreciate as well. Perhaps the Friday-like character's innocence allowed him to be more realistic without being always negative.

Christopher Reeve, who wrote the autobiographical book *Nothing Is Impossible: Reflections on a New Life*, was an amazing actor who played various roles in different kinds of movies. Unfortunately, while participating in an equestrian competition, he was thrown from his horse and became permanently paralyzed.

He could have subsequently become depressed for the rest of his life; instead, his positive attitude and determination helped him to overcome his physical disability in order to improve himself as well as to inspire others to pursue their goals, no matter their circumstances.

Grant Korgan wrote an autobiographical book called *Two Feet Back*. He was involved in a very bad snowmobiling accident. Even with his many trials and tribulations, both physically and emotionally, he remained positive. The people around him were very encouraging and supportive of his desire to improve himself. As a result, he chose to focus on his desire to improve himself physically and emotionally and to become a positive role model for other people in need of inspiration to help them rise above their circumstances by giving workshop presentations.

Another example that shows how being sensitive and having an upbeat attitude can result in a positive shift in one's perspective about life is a movie called *Room* with Brie Larson and Jacob Tremblay. Brie Larson, who won the Academy Award for best actress for this movie, plays the mother, with Jacob Tremblay cast in the role of her son. They are imprisoned in a backyard shed for many years.

In order to cope with this horrible situation, the mother does her very best to inspire him so that he can cope without questioning where they are. She helps him to enjoy his life as well as possible, although they eventually succeed in escaping to a better life.

Had she not been positive, sensitive, and determined to escape their imprisonment, both of them would probably have passed away due to their confinement.

The last example is that of a young adult who turned to gangs. This young adult and his younger brother eventually were put in the custody of their grandfather who raised them in their preteen and teen years in order to avoid the negative influence of gangs.

When the older brother entered high school, he took film production as an elective class. The teacher inspired him to be involved with various film projects, and the older brother became very enthusiastic. He and a fellow student eventually won two different young adult film competitions in their region, and a newspaper article in his community was devoted to the two of them.

I encountered and helped both of these brothers by giving them attention and validating them as individuals. I tutored Spanish to the older brother for a while; I even took the two of them and their grandfather on day trips.

Along with his very creative side, he helped out in his community with much younger kids, acting as a very good role model to his fellow students.

Upon graduating from high school, he entered a university in a specialized program designed for music and film, and he even went to China to learn more about film and music along with learning about a different culture.

While the older brother could have gone down the road of violence with a gang, he learned with the love, the compassion, the care, and the attention of family members, friends, and teachers that he could rise above his previous circumstances. In fact, he has been able to inspire others to better themselves as well.

His younger brother successfully completed his high school education and also has a very good attitude about life and a good work ethic.

Thus, while one cannot change the past, people have the opportunity, the right, and the responsibility to change their present with the hope of creating a much better future.

Motivation needs to originate from within the individual as much as possible and then oftentimes is augmented by interaction with role models, such as family members, friends, teachers, and community members, so that individuals feel inspired to have a positive purpose in life that will not only help them but perhaps others around them as well.

Young adults may have experienced many hardships and become hardened, but they can transcend these conditions to become more positive human beings with inspiration given by different people. Perhaps, the challenge of such hardened individuals could be the very reason why positive adults are inspired to work with them.

So, what are the essential ingredients to becoming more sensitive to youth, no matter what their pasts might have been? How do teachers acquire that delicate balance of being very aware of students while still completing the goals of the class? The rest of this chapter is going to be devoted specifically to answering those very questions.

Above and beyond the methods already discussed, another way for teachers to show that they care about their students as individuals is to develop a student information sheet with pertinent information such as email addresses, phone numbers, birthdays, special concerns, and any medical information at the beginning of the school year. This could be a first assignment to be completed by the next school day.

Upon turning in these student information sheets, teachers need to review them in detail in order to have a better understanding of their students as individuals and any special concerns they may have.

Whether young or old, it is nice to be recognized on one's birthday in one way or another, and most people appreciate being acknowledged with at least a simple "Happy Birthday."

Students especially like to have some sort of recognition, but they do not necessarily want to make it a big deal. Thus, one particularly important piece of information in order to connect with students on an emotional level is to record their birthdates. Whatever method teachers use to document their students' birthdays, be it on their technological device or on paper, when their birthday takes place, it can be handled in one of two ways.

If their birthday falls on a day that there is a quiz, a test, or a project due, it is definitely something they do not want to do, although they will begrudgingly complete it. After all, they more than likely wish to celebrate instead of having to deal with a graded assignment of any kind.

In the event that a graded assignment is due on their birthday, in order to honor them, it is suggested that they earn extra credit with either additional points or an increase to their grade, such as raising a B+ to an A− on their graded assignment. More than likely, they will feel that they are being honored, thus lessening the possibility of discipline issues.

If no graded assignment is due on their birthday during the school year, teachers may simply and quietly say something to them in order to honor them for another year on their special day. If they choose to take an extra quiz either before or after school on their special day when it is convenient for both teachers and students, students earn extra points or have their grade advanced as previously explained.

When a student's birthday falls on a weekend or during a vacation, it is suggested that this be documented so that when there is a graded assignment that falls on the number of their birthdate, they can earn extra points or extra credit. For example, if their birthday falls on July 2, since there typically is no school then, these students could earn extra points or extra credit on a school day, such as November 2.

For teachers who respect students and are sensitive to their needs, tact is extremely important when dealing with human emotions, especially when students are struggling academically. A teacher who is emotionally abusive by saying, "See, you aren't any good at that. Why waste your time being in this class?" clearly risks deflating the student's self-confidence, creating an environment in which he or she is unable to feel good and will likely develop a poor attitude. Although such negative comments may be hyperbole, there have been instances in which somewhat similar comments have been very devastating to some students.

While some people learn how to cope at an earlier age, most students, given an explosive situation of teachers being derogatory, will react in any number of ways, such as becoming angry, crying, or feeling so deflated that they totally lose any sense of respect for themselves and for their teachers.

Let's face it. We as adults do not want to be treated in a negative way. Students who are young adults deserve to be treated humanely and fairly as well. Unfortunately, some teachers believe that "if we could take being treated negatively and still manage to succeed when we were younger, then our students should be able to deal with adversity as well. They will survive." Such a rationale does not promote learning or help to improve students' self-worth, and it will likely limit chances for the development of positive relationships between students and teachers.

Students who encounter this sort of attitude in the classroom may ultimately share their concerns with other students, their parents, other teachers, and administrators, which could easily result in some kind of confrontation or disciplinary action against the teachers involved. Meetings are the best way to resolve such issues, although the students involved and their parents may want to make some sort of change in the class schedule so that such negative comments are avoided in the future. If the administration is unable to resolve the issue, students and their parents have the right to seek legal counsel in order to remedy the situation.

A student benefits from encouraging words like: "Yes, you did try your best, and I am sorry that happened. What could you have done differently? Have you considered . . . ? What if you . . . ?" Such comments and questions are much more sensitive, helpful, and constructive for correcting whatever the issues may be, and may help to improve their methods of studying, and ultimately their grades as well.

A great way to help underachieving students is to request that they meet with their teachers either before or after school. In such meetings, it is essential that teachers begin by saying: "How may I help you?" This allows students to feel that they have ownership of these meetings. They are more than likely going to feel comfortable expressing what the real issues are in terms of understanding the challenging material. This method of giving personal attention and being able to listen without judging reduces the possibility of discipline problems in the classroom.

A really very important way to bond with students personally is to be humorous. When teachers show their sense of humor without being condescending, students may laugh at what teachers say, or they may just cringe and think to themselves that they are really strange. No matter what their reactions, students may feel less stress and be more willing to learn instead of finding the subjects boring.

Unfortunately, bullying can occur at any time on social media or in person. Bullies take out their anger and vent their frustrations on others, sometimes with horrible consequences. Some victims of bullying tragically take their own lives, unable to bear the horrible treatment and humiliation. Bullies themselves may be ostracized by others in school; some are even charged with crimes and found guilty in a court of law.

A movie very worthy of your time and consideration is *The Gift*. It deals with the prolonged side effects of bullying by a bully and his companions on a meek boy. When the bully and his companions decide to harass him, the meek boy justifiably feels threatened. Unfortunately, instead of resisting, he accepts the cruelty of these people out of fear and not wanting to have anything worse be imposed upon him.

Years later, the previously bullied man encounters the man who was and still is a bully and who is now married. Without becoming angry, the previously bullied man is able to eventually make the bully realize how horrible he was, and still is, although it takes a lot of time and a serious reality check for the bully before this is accomplished.

Anyone who bullies needs help to deal with their own insecurities, ideally through counseling. It may or may not be appropriate for bullies to apologize directly to their victims, but they will need to make a genuine effort to demonstrate remorse and to show by their ongoing actions that they are worthy of being trusted. Even so, their victims may not want any kind of relationship at all with them, and they may never forgive them.

Individual counseling is important for both bully and victim. Those who have been bullied need to learn how to cope and how to defend themselves against such harassment in the future. Counseling can also help them to regain their self-confidence. Bullies need individual counseling to explore why they are abusive and to understand the deep-rooted, emotional causes for their behavior. They need to address these issues in order to feel better about themselves and to become more sensitive to others and their feelings.

If agreed upon by the bullied, the bullies, and their parents, in some instances, a group meeting with the counseling staff may be helpful to assess the dynamics of the situation in hopes of preventing such negative behavior in the future.

There is another great way for those who are being bullied to get help. "I Can Help" is a national organization (https://icanhelpline.org) that can be a great resource where people can learn how to resolve problems that surface in social media. There are trained professionals who will listen to young adults' situations and suggest different ways and resources to overcome any issues that bullies impose upon them.

Young adults usually learn from their parents how to be respectful, although there are those students who do not make the association that what they practice in their homes should be done in the classroom as well as in society. Of course, if they are unruly at home, it is very possible that they will act the same way in the classroom, although students usually know which teachers they can test and which ones demand their respect.

There are also students who still need to learn that it is appropriate to raise their hand when they wish to be recognized and when they have questions. Shouting for their teachers' attention over another student and while the rest of the class is busy with something is inappropriate behavior. In these circumstances, teachers then need to tactfully and respectfully mold such behavior into better behavior for the sake of common courtesy to everyone in the classroom. Student questions deserve answers when the time is right. Students also need to be sensitive and respectful of the other students and the teachers in the classroom.

While a majority of students are respectful of their teachers' knowledge and reputation, oftentimes there are a few students who believe they know more than their teachers. In turn, teachers are tested in terms of their knowledge, patience, and tolerance. Granted, such behaviors occurred before technology, although it seems as though it may be much more prevalent now.

For example, with the influx of technology and the ability to access information via any number of websites and apps, students expect to acquire information very quickly. When they do not quickly understand a concept, or if they are unable to apply what they have learned quickly, there are students who will become frustrated. They will want to give up. They will become irritated with the fact that they need more time to learn the information better.

While this typically happens with average or below-average students, above-average students tend to accept the challenge and will delve more deeply to understand and to apply what they need to know because they know that education does require time and patience and that it is not instantaneously acquired.

In turn, teachers have all kinds of students with varied levels of ability and interest so it can be challenging to answer all of their questions effectively so that they can learn, understand, perhaps appreciate, and successfully use the different aspects of the subject matter in their classwork, their homework, and their graded assignments. If the classes contain quality, respectful students, this is what makes teaching a dream come true.

When teachers encounter students who create discipline problems, placing them close to the teachers can be an option, because they will then know that the teachers mean business. Otherwise, they could ask them to stay for a minute or two after class in order to discuss their behavior. Sometimes this works and sometimes it doesn't. It all depends on the approach that the teachers use as well as the attitude of both the teachers and the students involved.

As a teacher, I had a very challenging student who continuously misbehaved in the classroom, and patience, encouragement, praise, tact, and respect never seemed to work to motivate her to change her attitude.

Years later on Facebook, I received a message from this former student. She apologized profusely for her previously negative attitude without explaining why she had acted that way. Her apology was accepted, although it was perplexing why she revealed this many years later. It turned out that she had decided to become a high school teacher, and she had been encountering students who behaved exactly as she had herself when she was younger and in my class. So, after realizing her own errors, she contacted me in order to ultimately get help. The end result was that the two of us met in order to discuss what was going on in her classroom with me giving her practical advice as to how to handle such students.

Years later, a former student revealed to her now-retired teacher that she was a "holy terror" in her other classes, although she always cooperated fully with this particular teacher. Puzzled, the teacher asked her why she had treated her differently. She responded that, while it was tempting to misbehave, this teacher treated her like an adult-in-training by being patient, help-ful, and always listening, thus gaining her respect.

Thus, while an educational background is a very important part of the classroom equation, social skills are also important to have and to practice in order to get along well with others, with both the very positive and the very negative students and anyone else in the educational community.

Teachers need to respect their students' individual differences so that they can be reached academically as much as possible. Indeed, this is a challenge, although if there is going to be harmony in the classroom and in the school environment, such a practice will be enormously beneficial for all concerned in our global community that thrives on uniqueness and unity.

Teachers have a certain amount of material that needs to be covered, and students need to learn that information to the best of their ability. While this is standard, the methods of instruction are varied. Having websites, apps, homework, and projects can facilitate learning. It is also suggested that open-ended questions and activities be included to enhance critical thinking and creative thinking. Perhaps, these kinds of thinking activities will lead to the desired educational results in some unusual ways that are very inspirational for all concerned. These kinds of activities can also promote self-respect and mutual respect.

In terms of encouraging students to listen to one another, thus enhancing mutual respect in the classroom, there are two books that can be very helpful. If teachers have completed their lesson plans on a given day, these books offer very good filler activities to use at the end of their classes in order to see how students respond, for students to learn how to become better listeners, and to be more respectful of one another's opinions.

The first book is entitled *The Kids' Book Of Questions* by Gregory Stock, specifically designed for preteens and teens. This book contains many hypo-thetical questions in which there is no right or wrong answer. It is best for the students to select a number. Then the teacher needs to determine if the question is appropriate. For instance, "If you were the principal of this school, what change would you make?"

This kind of hypothetical, open-ended question and others like it are good for young adults. When young adults are given the opportunity to state how they feel based on a situation, it makes them think critically and creatively, in order to possibly resolve the presented situations.

In the meantime, everyone needs to listen to what is said. They need to have the free reign to think and to gain self-confidence. They need to express how they feel about the presented situations. Other students need to listen to their logic and to their ideas without criticism. Ultimately, this activity can help build self-esteem for young adults. It can help to build respect amongst the students themselves. It can also help teachers to better understand how their students think.

The second book for consideration is entitled *The Book of Questions*, also by Gregory Stock, specifically designed for adults although, based on the age of the students, there are many questions found here that may be useful for discussion. The teacher should ask the students again for a number, and the teacher needs to determine whether or not the questions are appropriate for their age group. Again, everyone needs to listen to everyone else.

Such books can be very helpful to overcome the shyness that many young adults feel, although the amount of time will vary with each individual based on their past experiences, their maturity, and their desire to express their opinions.

KEY IDEAS TO REMEMBER

- Students learn from their successes and from their failures.
- Teachers need to be tactful and respectful to help their students.
- Parents of all kinds have many challenging roles to fulfill.
- Parents need to be sensitive to their young adults.
- Student attitudes affect their learning.
- Teachers need to be respectful of their students in order to change their attitudes.
- Teachers need to be motivating.
- Being a bully or being bullied needs to be addressed in sensitive ways.
- Teachers need to respect their students' differences while completing class goals.

Chapter Ten

Some Successful Methods of Teaching

In terms of the information that needs to be learned, when students are presented with totally new concepts it is always a good idea for teachers to estimate how much time it will take for them to learn the material through practice in class and by doing homework. Asking leading questions can be very helpful, along with asking students if they have questions in order to alleviate any stress that they may be feeling. Teachers are thus demonstrating patience and letting students know that they are receptive to their questions.

For example, when foreign language teachers have covered the regular verb forms in the present tense and then plan to introduce irregular verb forms that basically have the same endings that students should already be familiar with, it is a good idea to verify what they have already learned by giving them an exercise that shows the teachers that the students know the previous information well enough to proceed. If they do not, this is the appropriate time to reinforce previous concepts before presenting a new concept that has similar patterns.

When the students are presented with new information that has some of the same basic patterns, not only will they see the logic in what is being presented, they will also feel much more confident with and more open about the new material. They will feel more positive and more receptive to learning, and there may even be less likelihood of classroom discipline issues.

One way to actively involve students, with the teachers being the facilitators, is by having students learn a certain amount of information and then, for homework, asking that the students write down three questions with answers. The next day, the teachers check off that this assignment has been completed.

Next, the students stand up from their seats and get into two rows facing one another, with the first row classified as A and the second row classified as B. If there are an odd number of students such as thirty-five instead of thirty-four, then the thirty-fifth student is in row A.

The A row of students ask the B row of students their questions, and the B row of students answer the questions. Then the B row of students ask their questions with the A row of students answering them. As for the odd-numbered student in the A row, he or she asks an additional set of questions of the students in the B row. In the meantime, the teachers roam outside the rows to listen to the questions and to the answers, and they clarify and answer any additional questions posed by the students.

Upon completing the two sets of questions from the A and B rows of students, the B row students pass to their right in order to answer a new set of questions. The B row students at the end of the row go to the front of the line to meet the A row students. After completing all of the questions by all of the students, the students return to their desks, and the teachers ask if there are any additional questions. After doing so, the teachers proceed with the rest of the lesson plan.

Such an activity empowers students to become more knowledgeable and more confident about the material they need to learn. The students are also able to get up from their seats and move around, and that can help those students who may easily fall asleep in class at different times.

As far as assignments are concerned, there is a lot of debate. Some people believe that the classroom is good enough for learning, that students do not need any homework. Some people go to the opposite extreme, believing that the more homework students have above and beyond the classroom, the more it will help them. Both points of view have their merits.

Indeed, the classroom does offer a lot of opportunity for learning. Perhaps teachers can condense some materials so that the overall concepts are learned. In this way, students can have a life after school for whatever they please.

There are teachers who believe that there is only so much that can be introduced in the classroom because there is so much more to learn. Thus, teachers assign their students homework to continue learning the information. If this approach is taken, it is best not to assign an excessive amount of homework. If students are given a few exercises that will allow them to learn specific concepts, that is all that is really needed.

If students are given pages upon pages of homework based on a single concept, this may result in "overkill." There comes a point at which students know the concepts with a minimum amount of exercises and effort. If there is "overkill" with the same concepts, this can result in the students being "turned off" by the amount of work required.

A notable exception for which a lot of homework and exercises are usually necessary is for Advanced Placement classes, due to the intensity of the material and the prospect of taking and hopefully passing the Advanced Placement exams. This extra effort can result in these students earning higher grade point averages (GPA) in their high schools, possibly contending for the valedictorian and the salutatorian status of their graduating class, and possibly earning college credits based on their Advanced Placement exam scores.

Typically when teachers identify errors, their natural tendency is to correct the errors. It is suggested instead that they underline or circle the errors. For example, if there is an incorrect spelling of a word, underline or circle the word. The assignments are returned to the students who review them. Next, the students explain their errors to the teacher and determine what the correct answers should be. It is a good idea to give another assignment to the rest of the class in order for them to continue learning.

Another way to actively engage students when their work needs to be corrected and evaluated is for teachers to sit with each of the students while they are grading their work. In the process of doing so, teachers and students are encouraged to ask questions and to make comments. Of course, it takes time to do this, but it truly can be beneficial for the students so that they can understand what they have done correctly and incorrectly. Again, it is then a good idea to give another assignment for the rest of the class in order for them to continue learning.

In this way, the students are evaluating the quality of their answers while the teacher evaluates their answers and determine their grades. If students understand what the correct answers need to be, fine. This can be just as helpful as the teacher presenting information for the first time. If the students do not understand the corrections, there can be a discussion between the teacher and the student at this time. This is again another good learning experience for the student.

Many teachers like to allow their students to study bits and pieces of the information in groups. In turn, students give group presentations. These presenters feel empowered with this information and may feel good that they are able to share it with others. The presenters and the other students may learn much more from one another. The role of the teacher during such presentations is that of a listener on the side or in the back of the classroom. The teacher should not interrupt the presenters but rather explain anything the presenters may not have understood completely or that needs to be expanded upon at the end of the presentations.

The presenters should ask the student audience whether or not they have any questions and answer their questions to the best of their ability. If they are unable to do so, the teacher needs to answer the questions. Also, the presenters should give a practice quiz to the student audience in order to see how much they actually understand.

There are many benefits and disadvantages of group presentations. So much depends upon the personalities of the students involved, their attitudes about group presentations, the actual information itself—if it is relatively easy to understand or if it is rather challenging for students to understand by themselves—and also how the teacher wishes to structure the method of the group presentations.

It is important for teachers to be sensitive and consider that some students may have misgivings about this method of instruction. There are those who may feel less than confident about themselves or the presented information. They may feel very threatened and scared by having to be in front of the class with their peers looking at them and perhaps being hypercritical. While teachers truly do control how the subject matter is presented, they need to determine when teacher presentations and group presentations are the most desirable.

Veteran teachers are valuable resources for new teachers. Discussing different teaching techniques is a great way to collaborate and to learn from one another. In this way, teachers can choose those techniques that they feel comfortable enough to use and that will benefit their own students.

Teaching, taking into account student differences and teachers having high expectations, is like juggling. Teachers always need to be aware of each of the students, the overall goals of the class, and how much material can be realistically covered during each grading period in order to have the students remain on task as much as possible. It does take a lot of time, a lot of organization, a lot of practice, a lot of tact, a lot of patience, a lot of encouragement, a lot of praise, and mutual respect in order to achieve the goals of the class.

KEY IDEAS TO REMEMBER

- Teachers need to realistically judge time for classroom activities for their students.
- There is a lot of debate about the importance of homework.
- Group presentations by students can be beneficial for learning.
- Teaching, taking into account student differences and teachers having high expectations, is like juggling.

Chapter Eleven

The Process of Studying

Teachers are a very important part of the educational process. They develop lesson plans that are intended to enhance student learning in the classroom. They also do a tremendous amount of work to evaluate student performance in order to give the most accurate grades, and they have to contend with student issues. Teachers do their best to reach out to students by encouraging them and by praising them when it is warranted.

Outside the classroom environment, many teachers communicate with their students in order to be accessible via texts and emails so that students can consult them with regard to homework responsibilities or if they need help understanding the subject matter.

The other part of the equation of the educational process is placed on the students themselves, if they want to learn to the best of their ability. Students will oftentimes hear their teachers say that they are to study a certain amount of information by the next school day. Teachers give explanations and practice assignments so that students will feel more comfortable with the information. Students will have homework, a sort of "dry run," in order to learn the information. Teachers frequently refer them to websites and apps, developed by textbook companies or others, that can also aid them in their studies. Even with all of these supports for learning, students still need to study the material and to complete the assignments in a timely and consistent manner, and it is especially important to apply what they have learned. When they do, they are more apt to feel good about the studied and practiced information.

Students want to devote time to their own hobbies, to their smartphones to play games or to use social media, to participate in sports, or to go to work, so they are often impatient and try to complete their homework assignments quickly. Nevertheless, if students choose to rush through their assignments, they are more likely to make mistakes and they may not be learning as much as they could.

When they come to the realization that they need to take their time in order to fully understand and appreciate the material, and in order to apply the information learned currently and in the future, they may also be more successful in completing their work, and they may even earn higher grades in their classes, which is usually their top priority.

While many students have developed good study tools for themselves, there are those young adults who have not developed successful learning techniques and have consistently earned lower grades due to any number of reasons, and they may consequently feel like failures.

Thus, if young adults have study habit issues and wish to improve their learning and their grades, the following ideas are worthy to recommend:

- It is important to consider grade goals. If you wish to earn As in all of your classes or at least in a majority of them, you need to realistically determine what you are willing to do on a regular basis in order to earn those grades. It is a good idea to write a chart of each class with the grades you wish to earn along with what specifically you will do each day. It is then important for you to display this chart where you can see it each day so that you can refer to it as a reminder for yourself.
- How much time do you study on a regular basis? If you study an average of twenty minutes a day without feeling satisfied with your grades, please consider studying an average of thirty minutes a day. It is also a good idea to write down the number of minutes on your grade goal chart.
- Never consider cramming, expecting to learn everything all at once. It takes a lot of time and a lot of practice on a daily basis. Also, you are apt to retain the information studied and practiced much longer, which will help you to improve your performance on future assignments, quizzes, tests, and final exams.
- If your grades are suffering and if you are involved with outside activities such as sports, clubs, work, and/or hobbies, all of which can require a lot of your time, it is to your advantage to reduce or to eliminate some of these extra activities. Granted, such activities are worthwhile as a way to relieve stress. Nevertheless, if such activities take too much time and

actually interfere with your education, it will be to your detriment because your education is highly important now and for your future.

- Many students feel compelled to study a lot in order to earn high grades along with being involved in extra activities that they hope will look good on their résumés when it comes to applying for scholarships, grants, loans, colleges, and universities. While having extra activities looks good, it will not be of any benefit if you are exhausted due to a chronic lack of sleep that causes your grades to become lower.
- Where do you study? Do you need an area where you have no distractions? If so, if your grades are not where you wish them to be, perhaps you need to consider having fewer distractions.
- If you need to listen to music while you are studying, you may wish to wear earbuds to play some music, preferably classical music, because classical music may help you concentrate better. If you prefer more modern music, it needs to be music that will allow you to concentrate better without being too much of a distraction.
- If you have many distractions around you, like noise or a big family, if at all possible, you may wish to study with your door closed. If there are so many distractions in your home that you are unable to concentrate, you may wish to study at a friend's home, at a library, or at a café.
- Related to distractions, a very important consideration is viewing social media and text messages on a regular basis while completing your assignments. You need to weigh how important they are. No matter how much you wish to connect with your friends, remember that they too have assignments to complete as well as to study. Of course, if there is a true emergency, it should be addressed promptly. Otherwise, it can wait.
- If you study by yourself, so be it, provided that you are very successful.
- If you study by yourself and if you earn low grades, it can be a good idea to work either with a friend or in a study group. If it works, fine. If it does not work, it is a good idea to involve yourself with another friend or with another study group, provided that you can focus on your studies.

After having considered all of these recommendations, it is time to examine your actual study methods. If you have not already incorporated them, please consider the following ideas that may improve your chances of understanding the information you need to learn and ultimately help you to earn higher grades:

- Please go to https://www.quizlet.com in order to develop flash cards so that you can use them on your smartphone or tablet. On the other hand, if the textbook company has an accompanying website or app, it may provide flash cards already.
- Please consider reading out loud. The reason for saying what you are learning out loud is because you are seeing it, you are reading it, and you are hearing what you are saying. You may be able to better remember what you have said to yourself as a result.
- After studying the information, if you are able to understand everything, that is ideal. If you are unable to understand everything, it is a good idea to write down your questions. Then, you may wish to discuss those questions with a classmate.
- If it gets to the point that you truly do not understand the material very well and if your grades are dropping, please consider working with a peer tutor through your counseling center, if available.
- After studying the information and discussing your questions with a classmate, if you still have no definitive answers, it is then time to ask the teacher. Granted, doing so may or may not be easy. Generally speaking, teachers are glad to answer questions when you and they have the time to do so, in person or via email or text if they give you their contact information.
- If you feel hesitant to ask the teachers due to their personalities or due to how you get along with them, consider the following. There is no such thing as a stupid question. It is only stupid if it is not asked. In other words, you are in the classes to learn, and your teachers are there to help you learn. It is your right and your responsibility to learn, and it is their responsibility to help you learn. So take the initiative to ask for help because they are there for that reason.
- If teachers give questions that will actually be on the graded assignment, it is best to include studying these hints or questions in detail so that you have a better chance of succeeding on the graded assignment.
- Perhaps, with your parents' permission, a tutor could be hired through the nationwide tutoring website WyzAnt at https://www.wyzant.com or any other reputable tutoring company.
- If money is a factor and your parents are unable to afford to hire a tutor from such a company, you may be able to locate a tutor through your local library or at your local college or university. Contact them and they can lead you to the appropriate people, if they are available. You may be able

to find a volunteer tutor or at least one who charges less for their services in comparison to a tutoring company.

Understand that not every subject is going to be easy for everybody. We all have our strengths and weaknesses. It is what we do in order to overcome any weaknesses that counts. As John Donne stated, "No man is an island." We are a community of helpers. There is always help available. Occasionally, a class may be just too much of a challenge, resulting in only frustration instead of a joy of learning and a sense of accomplishment. When this is the case, it may be appropriate to make a change in classes, if it is permitted to do so.

KEY IDEAS TO REMEMBER

- Teacher communication with parents can be more productive when conducted in person.
- Students need to study the material and to complete their assignments.
- Successful study habits can result in more successes.
- If students want to improve their grades, different approaches need to be considered.

Chapter Twelve

The Very Competitive Side of Education

Indeed, we definitely do live in a very competitive world of education. Miklos Fejer, who is a language consultant in Japan, stated that "healthy competition motivates us to evolve and transcend." We can learn from one another. We can help one another. We can become more informed. Our society can thus become better overall.

Starting in kindergarten, school districts encounter parents who are extremely competitive and want only the best for their children. While this is natural, some parents take it to the extreme. They find out about certain elementary schools that have waiting lists, oftentimes with applicants waiting for years, because they offer a curriculum that is very well-structured and focuses on advanced academics.

Another reason many elementary schools become very popular and in demand is due to the fact that the majority of the teachers there, if not all of them, are highly respected on account of their personalities along with their ability to successfully teach their students. As a result, the test scores of these elementary schools typically are very high, all of which makes them more appealing to parents.

In such elementary schools, the demands are exceedingly high so that the students learn the material very thoroughly. They are given many hours of homework during weekdays, over the weekend, and on vacations. Parents who are able to do so will devote countless hours to helping their children in their homes. If the parents cannot afford the time to work with their children, they will oftentimes hire tutors to work with their children. With such high standards required by these elementary schools and such high hopes of the parents, it is expected that the children will become much more knowledgeable than the average elementary students of other schools.

Sports will always be an integral part of both the elementary and high school educational experience. There are many kinds of sports for students to participate in. If they have been in these sports in previous years, they more than likely will want to continue to perfect their skills. This will require many hours of conditioning depending upon the sport, many hours of practice, and many hours involved in the games themselves. Along with the amount of time involved, there can be a lot of prestige and a lot of satisfaction earned, not only on the school site level, but also in the area.

By devoting so much time to these sports and as their popularity increases, there is a very good likelihood that students may be evaluated by college and university coaches for their athletic performance. An extra enticement to continue participation in sports can be that student athletes may be able to earn scholarships in order to offset some, if not all, of the expenses involved in attending an institution of higher education. As a result, there are many parents who encourage their children to develop and to perfect their athletic skills from early on.

One caution needs to be taken. Parents need to realize that while perfecting their offspring's athletic abilities can be very good for their overall health, there are unfortunately accidents that do happen that can hinder or stop their child's ability to participate in sports. Thus, it is best to have a balance of a good, solid athletic ability along with a good, solid academic ability, with academic education taking priority over athletics, especially if their offspring's grades are low.

Along with high academic standards, teachers and parents strongly encourage these youngsters to become involved in many kinds of competitive games against other schools that may or may not be regarded as high-quality elementary schools. Group competitions, such as the Science Olympiad (https://soinc.org), math competitions, the Academic Pentathlon primarily for the middle/junior high school level (http://www.ocde.us/pentathlon), the Academic Decathlon specifically for the high school level (http://www.usad.org), and debates, for example, can easily generate goodwill, harmony, respect, confidence, and learning all at once.

The Science Olympiad students typically work with their teachers during class time along with meeting before and after school in order to experiment on unique, creative ideas. In turn, they find out what works well and what needs to be revised as needed. Upon completing their science projects, they compete against other schools with their unique science projects. This is a great opportunity for teachers and parents to support their young adults and for students to meet other students from other schools. It is thus truly a very positive experience overall.

Both the Academic Pentathlon and the Academic Decathlon consist of art, history, science, language, literature, music, mathematics, social science, essay, economics, and a general theme for that school year. The Academic Decathlon studies also include how to interview, how to prepare and to present an organized speech, and how to prepare for impromptu speaking.

Coaches throughout the United States learn what the specific topics, which change every year, will be in advance so that they can study them during the course of a year. The selection process of the teams is based on the students' grades, and includes A, B, and C students, along with an evaluation of their motivation, desire, and attitude. Many school administrations allow these teams to have their own classes, if scheduling will permit it and if the students can fit this class in their regular schedules.

Events consist of different school teams competing against one another at the county level, and the excitement is an amazing experience for the participating students, for their schools, for the parents, and for the coaches.

The Academic Pentathlon competition is typically a one- or two-day event at the county level with the bragging rights for that county, and there are regional and national competitions for the subsequent winners.

The Academic Decathlon competition is usually a two-day event at the county level with the winning team advancing to meet other county winners at the state level. In turn, the state-level winners compete against other state winners for the national championship.

There are other competitions, such as debates, speech competitions, mock trials, agricultural competitions, and art competitions that allow students to use their strengths in order to try to become the top winners.

Generally speaking, such motivated students tend to want to take classes in high school as ninth and tenth graders that challenge them. Such classes are Honors English, world languages, advanced math, and even cultural anthropology, for example. When students take honors classes and excel, there is a better likelihood that they will be recommended to take Advanced Placement (AP) classes in eleventh and twelfth grades.

These students are typically recommended by their teachers, although there are high schools that will allow any student who knows about the challenges to take these classes. If they are consistently successful in meeting the challenges of these classes, they continue to advance through the curriculum and oftentimes thrive. Otherwise, depending upon the individual students themselves, they may need to be placed into other classes that are still a challenge for them, but where the stress is not as significant.

One advantage of these advanced-level classes is that there tend to be fewer disciplinary problems so that teachers are educators rather than a combination of educators and disciplinarians. Students who were previously in classes with the general student population where there may have been more discipline problems frankly can find themselves relieved by not having to be irritated by such students.

In order to earn an A in AP classes, students are required to meet very strict curriculum guidelines and timelines so teachers must assign many hours of homework during the week, during the weekends, during vacations during the school year, and even during the summer months.

Oftentimes, students who are motivated to attend college, or those who feel obligated to attend college due to their parents and their families, will take several AP classes each school year. They can become overburdened with a lot of work, unless they like the subjects and the teachers. For others, it can truly be a joy of learning that motivates them instead of just a need to complete the required coursework.

Another advantage of taking AP classes is the opportunity for students to take the AP exams. If they score high enough on these exams, they can earn college credits, thus allowing them to take fewer classes while attending college. These students, their teachers, their parents, and the school administration will be delighted by high scores and pleased with students' achievements. Also, for students and their parents, any college credits earned mean less money to be expended for college tuition.

While many AP students do very well on their AP exams, there are those who know the information but have a "bad day" and do not do as well as they would like. Others may feel overwhelmed by the abundance of exam questions to answer in the time given. In other words, many factors can result in lower scores. It is thus suggested that once the students feel prepared for the AP exams, it is best to take them during their junior year of high school. If exams need to be taken again, students have another opportunity during their senior year.

If and when students need more personal attention or if they need to consult an expert, parents who can afford it will hire a tutor from a nearby college campus or from a tutoring company, such as WyzAnt. More often than not, these students will ultimately understand the information better and earn higher grades.

Students who have taken more challenging classes, such as AP classes, and who are actively involved in extracurricular activities will be regarded more highly for scholarships, grants, and loans, and by colleges and universities for admission. Many such students and their parents oftentimes set their goals quite high so that they become almost too focused on the goal of attending their desired college or university. If they achieve their desired goals, that is all well and good. Due to a lot of competition, there can be letdowns due to not being selected. It is thus advisable for students to determine and to prioritize three different institutions of higher learning. The ultimate goal of earning any monies for a college or a university and to attend the desired institution is to eventually earn the most-desired degree from the best or better college or university that will bring with it prestige and ultimately the career job they prefer.

On the other hand, there are many students who are unable or are unwilling to take challenging classes, such as AP classes. They may be unable to if they have not developed the study habits required for such demanding classes. Students may try to take them, and they may find them to be too demanding, thus requiring them to take general classes. They may be resigned to the fact that they are incapable of performing in such demanding classes, or they may simply be content to take the less demanding classes.

In such circumstances, it is important for parents to recognize that their high expectations of themselves, whether established themselves or perhaps prompted by their own parents, may not be suitable for their children. Their own offspring are different. This is not to label their offspring as "bad," it means accepting them as individuals with their own desires and abilities. It is best to allow them to become their own persons and to fulfill whatever will make them the most productive and happiest. After all, that is what parents really want for their children.

While competition can be a very healthy component of our lives so that we individually and as a global society can improve, there is a negative side that needs to be addressed that can occur in the classroom. If and when students become very frustrated by being unable to understand concepts of a subject and while there are many resources available to them such as teachers, fellow students, websites, apps, and tutors, there can be the temptation to want to cheat or to plagiarize.

While most students respect honesty and in turn practice honesty, there are those students who rationalize their actions to cheat. They may have an internal dialogue, saying that they didn't have enough time to study, that they didn't understand the information well enough, that they don't get along well enough with their teachers, or any number of other reasons in order to justify their actions. They will start looking at another student's quiz or test in order to get the right answers, or they may have the answers on their smartphone on their lap or on the seat. At the same time, they will constantly be aware of what the teachers are doing in order not to be caught.

Under such circumstances, it is only a matter of time until they are caught, and they will need to deal with the consequences of their actions based on the policies of both the school and the teacher in this regard. Then, it is best to accept the fact that they have done something wrong, to deal with the consequences, and to learn from such mistakes. To refute the obvious or to try to rationalize one's cheating only prolongs the inevitable, and they know they are wrong, no matter what they may wish to say.

When it comes to people who plagiarize, such behavior will also eventually be discovered. Many English teachers have their students submit essays through specific websites that can analyze whether part of or the entire essay is based on someone else's writings. When it is determined to have been written by someone else, the results will not be very appealing for the plagiarizer. Of course, the student will fail this assignment, and may incur other punishment that the school's policy and the teacher determine.

In order to try to prevent cheating and plagiarizing, I have discussed these self-defeating behaviors with students, along with suggesting positive behaviors in terms of studying. The students were asked if they wish their teachers to be honest, and the overriding answer was in the affirmative. Then, the students were tactfully told to be honest with themselves and with all teachers. Such a discussion is instrumental for a better classroom overall in terms of honesty.

While teachers try to teach to the best of their ability and eventually determine grades for their students, students can evaluate their teachers in a very unique way that can help other future students to have a better understanding of their upcoming teachers. The website Rate My Teachers (https://www.ratemyteachers.com) offers such an opportunity for students to give an impression of their teachers.

While this can be a very good way to evaluate teachers and to determine who is considered "good" or "bad," it always needs to be remembered that the personalities of both the teachers and the students are extremely important factors in how they relate to one another. If they get along well, there is a better opportunity of a more positive relationship. If they do not get along well, there is a better likelihood of a more negative experience overall. It is important to consider that the situations that arise will always be important factors in determining their relationships on a regular basis. Although such a website offers hearsay similar to that from friends who are older giving advice, students can get a better idea as to how these teachers interact.

The last but not least important factors to consider are that each student is different, each teacher is different, each situation is different. It is very possible that new combinations of people and new situations will present different outcomes. In other words, preconceived perceptions of people may affect how they feel and may influence situations. It is thus important that students, their parents, and teachers are open-minded so that the ultimate goal will be the students' education.

Bottom line, when teachers and students are respectful of one another, there is a sense of mutual respect and mutual trust, and the relationship between them is apt to be very positive and very productive.

KEY IDEAS TO REMEMBER

- School districts have parents who are extremely competitive and only want the best for their young adults.
- Athletic competitions are an integral part of the educational experience at both the elementary and high school levels.
- Group competitions, such as the Academic Pentathlon, the Academic Decathlon, and the Science Olympiad, can be very positive and energetic experiences that result in more learning, teach students how to work well with others, and promote self-esteem.
- Honors and AP classes are great for motivated students, although students need to be realistic if they feel stressed.
- Students can rate their teachers at https://www.ratemyteachers.com.

Chapter Thirteen

Easing the Stress of Education

While there are many ways that young adults can improve their understanding of any subject, it truly can become almost insurmountable for them. Granted, a subject can be presented in any number of creative, logical ways by teachers, peers, and online, from the simple to the complex, with exercises and practice quizzes in order to confirm learning.

When they are given a homework assignment during the week and if they do not complete it during class time, students often need to take care of other obligations prior to focusing on homework, such as sports and work. Then, they need to eat dinner. Finally, they need to begin working on homework assignments. If they are focused on social media, they are only delaying the inevitable to complete their work, thus creating their own stress, and that is definitely not what they want—more stress.

If and when they are assigned homework on a Friday for the next week, they need to consider the following. They have already had a full week with school and everything else they needed to do. They need and deserve a break! So, it is suggested that they relax—that Friday night be time to be by themselves, with family, or with friends.

Once Saturday arrives and when they do not have things to do, then is the time to begin working on whatever needs to be completed for the next week. By relaxing on Friday after school and by having more time on Saturday and perhaps on Sunday as needed, they will have a better opportunity to be thorough without being preoccupied with school's stringent schedule.

If they complete their homework on Saturday, it is suggested they spend Sunday with family and friends. Once Sunday evening arrives, it is a good idea to skim through what they have been assigned as homework. In this way, once Monday arrives, they will be refreshed as to what they had to do, and they will know what they will be dealing with in class on Monday.

Students may wish to wait until Sunday, if and only if they definitely know that the homework is minimal; however, this is not advisable, because it is very possible that it may take more time, and the last thing they wish to experience is more stress, and they more than likely will cram more, perhaps needing to stay up very late. The end result can easily be that they may learn less and have less sleep, both of which will affect their ability to understand the concepts very well during class on Monday.

While it can be reassuring to understand the material, when it comes time for the actual graded assignments, such as quizzes, tests, projects, and final exams, it may become very frightening and very nerve-wracking for them. Thus, stress to excel can be higher than the joy to learn.

In order to counteract the stress of graded assignments, it is important for students to understand what needs to be learned, and that is usually according to the textbook and the notes the teacher gives. When the teacher frequently emphasizes certain aspects of the material, it usually means this information will be on the graded assignments.

When the teacher gives a project to complete individually and when it is due in a week or more, they need to consider completing the rest of the homework for the rest of the classes first. Then, they can read and reread what the expectations are for the project. If and when they have questions, they need to ask the teacher for clarification. Then, they can develop ideas for this assigned project. When done consistently, they are more likely to feel satisfied with what has been developed, and they will tend to receive a higher grade on it, because they will have planned well to complete the project and hopefully they will experience little or no stress.

When the teacher assigns them to a group in order to complete a project, he or she will probably give them time in class to begin working on it. It is best to work together as much as possible. The more time they can focus on what needs to be done, the better the product will be. Granted, there will always be students who rely on more-studious, more-focused classmates, and it may be difficult or challenging to get them to be more involved. Perhaps, with encouragement and organization, they can determine what they can and will do so that they can be a part of the group. If it is a group project and if everyone in the group is going to earn the same grade, this can be a very good motivation so that everyone will wish to earn a higher grade.

Since teachers develop all kinds of graded assignments, such as quizzes, tests, and final exams, understanding the actual format can be very helpful to students in order to alleviate stress, even though they may feel comfortable about the material. If it is a multiple-choice type of graded assignment, it is suggested to, at first, disregard the possible answers. Then, they can determine what they believe is the answer. Afterward, they can select the best answer. Another possible way to approach such a graded assignment is that usually one or two answers are completely incorrect with the others being rather close to the actual answer.

If the graded assignments are fill-ins, it is very important to read the entire sentence in order to determine what the answer is. In this way, students will have a better, clearer understanding of what the correct answer is.

If the graded assignments are in the format of short paragraphs or essays, it is best to read the questions very well and to jot down some ideas in an outline form. Then students can rearrange the outline so that it makes good, logical sense. It should be remembered that teachers wish students to be clear and logical in their answers. If responses are confusing, the grade will be lower.

If students are good in spelling, grammar, and punctuation, this too will be helpful when it comes to short paragraph answers and/or essays, if they are take-home assignments. If students are not necessarily confident in these areas, it is best to check a website, like http://www.polishmywriting.com, where you can paste or compose a document. Then, you can get the appropriate feedback. Otherwise, on their technological device, they should be able to use autocorrect.

If students have issues specifically with spelling, it is best to go to http://www.spellingschool.com. If they have issues specifically with grammar, it is a good idea to go to https://www.grammarcheck.net. If they have difficulty specifically with punctuation, it will be of benefit to go to http://www.gingersoftware.com.

If they have an in-class essay to write and if they know some of the general questions that might be given, they might try answering some or all of these questions and then go to the above websites in order to check for spelling, grammar, and punctuation. While they cannot necessarily memorize everything, at least if they are aware of some or all of the errors they typically make, they then will have a better opportunity to write a better essay.

No matter what the format of the graded assignments, students need to study consistently in order to do well on them. It is like a hobby. It is best to take time on a regular basis so that they will be pleased with the final product. If they delay their studies and attempt to cram the night before the graded assignment, the chances are very high that the grade will be less than desired.

After having consistently studied the material over a given period of time, and if the quiz, test, or final exam is the next school day, it is very important to complete homework for the next school day. Then it is best to go to bed at a reasonable hour to get enough sleep and to feel rested. After all, if they are alert, they are apt to remember a lot more and are less apt to make mistakes.

Once it comes to the day of the actual quiz, test, or final exam, it is best to take a big, deep breath so that they can feel more relaxed. Then they can begin and complete this graded assignment with care. The operative words "with care" need to be emphasized, because it is easy to think that everything seems easy and that they simply need to complete this graded assignment so that they can relax again. Nevertheless, it is best to be thorough and read everything carefully so that they can answer everything correctly. It is also a good idea to check and recheck the answers in order to make sure the responses are correct. That is how they are going to be more successful without making errors.

As for wishing to complete a graded assignment quickly so that they can relax again, while it is understandable to feel that way, to rush through everything with the final goal of completing it will not necessarily help them to earn the highest possible grade. Studying the material, patiently and thoroughly, will help a student to be much more satisfied with the results.

Competition between siblings can create stress. If they assess each other as "smarter" or "less intelligent" than one another, or if they are told this by their parents, then there can be the added emotion of being considered superior or inferior, or "worthy" or "not worthy" of an education. Under these circumstances, a sibling considered to be "more intelligent" may have the added stress of having to continue to do excellent work, or they may become overconfident and conceited. The so-called less intelligent sibling can be stigmatized, feeling that they haven't met the goals that their parents have established or received the grades that their siblings have earned. As a result, they may not feel confident in their personal or professional lives. Either situation can have resounding and lasting effects for these individuals in the future.

Please consider this example. Parents, whose older son was getting my help for Spanish, once commented to me, in front of both the older son and the younger son, that the younger son was "smarter." Even if accurate, it was very disheartening for the older son to hear this statement. It likely caused discomfort for both siblings, and it also risked creating a sense of superiority in the younger son. It is extremely important to be tactful and respectful of siblings.

When parents consider their offspring as separate individuals without judging them, either covertly or overtly, when they genuinely praise them, and when they genuinely encourage them all without making comparisons or contrasts to anyone else, their offspring's self-respect and self-confidence will be improved and stress will be diminished. Students contend with enough pressure from other classmates. Of course, even without parents' labels, siblings may label themselves.

If this happens, parents definitely need to have a dialog with all of their children about the importance of each individual, noting that everyone has their own gifts and talents. It is then hoped that the offspring are given the opportunity to voice their feelings and to ease the competitiveness that can be present within a family with regard to education.

There are instances in which students have not fulfilled their own expec-tations or their parents' expectations to earn high enough grades, up through high school graduation. Some students become depressed. When parents note these feelings, it is best to discuss and validate these feelings as much as possible. Also, it is best to confirm that they as parents respect their kids' individualities.

Family conversations on a regular basis are advisable. Such meetings can help to alleviate stress and to improve family communication. Related to family conversations, it is also suggested that families have time together in order to talk about what is important for them. While siblings will usually just say everything is fine, it is best to delve more deeply into their day and their feelings. Again, as was mentioned in a previous chapter, the books *The Kids' Book of Questions* and *The Book of Questions* by Gregory Stock can be very helpful for families exploring ways to voice their views about issues that matter to them, and the side benefit will be that siblings may become more expressive.

If and when the parents notice that their kids need more help dealing with stress than they can provide, it is important for the parents and their kids to discuss with the school counselor what the possibilities are, as was already mentioned. It is also suggested that these students consider getting individual counseling in order to reveal and resolve any underlying issues.

No matter what kinds of expectations parents have for their offspring and no matter what kinds of comparisons and contrasts are made, students need to accept that there will be successes and failures. Successes are obviously more desirable and are easily acceptable. This signifies that a lot of learning has taken place, and it shows how time and work on a regular basis can help them to accomplish anything they wish, now and in the future.

Above-average, average, and below-average achievers will do well in society. Upon graduating from high school, some students will realize that they wish to further improve their education and opportunities for adult education or vocational education or attending a college or a university will be very good options to consider. In other words, education is not finite, and there is always something to learn. For instance, if we think about technology five or ten years ago, it is very different, meaning that different abilities need to be learned by everybody.

So, while the reality of our situation is that we live in a competitive world in which education is the gateway to a brighter financial future, people need to live up to their own potential and that takes some more time than others. Students need guidance—which teachers, classmates, websites, and apps can help to provide—although it is ultimately more important for people to feel good about themselves and to fulfill their own dreams in their own ways at their own time. Sometimes, however, a mentor can be the inspiration and the motivation that sets a student on the path to a possible career.

KEY IDEAS TO REMEMBER

- Planning to complete homework needs to be done in order to be more successful and to feel less stress.
- Understanding the format of the graded assignments, such as projects, quizzes, tests, and finals, will help the student to feel less stress.
- Reviewing the answers on graded assignments will help the student to earn higher grades.
- Parents need to be tactful and respectful of their young adults, because they all learn differently.
- Parents need to listen to their young adults.

Chapter Fourteen

Different Ways to Educate Without Being in School

Along with acquiring a formal education in a public, private, charter, online, or home school environment, there are many other opportunities available for families to have educational activities without homework, without grading, and without stress. In other words, there can be another way to experience the joy of learning.

If there are really young children in the home, going to a toy store can be very helpful to educate them while having fun. The labels on toys usually identify the most appropriate ages that the toys are good for. If there are any doubts as to its usefulness or as to its educational value, it is then best to talk it over with a store employee. Then the best decision can be made.

When parents bring the toys home, it is really important to work with the young kids so that they can fully appreciate the fun and the educational value that the toys can provide.

Nevertheless, not every single toy needs to have an educational component to it. It can simply be the joy of having fun, and it is very possible that such a joy can tap into their creativity in playing.

While it is customary to assign chores at home, when children are the appropriate age, it can be very interesting for them to help in the preparation of meals as well as learning how to clean up after the meals. Who knows? Such an activity can actually inspire them to want to cook on their own, to experiment with different kinds of foods, possibly becoming chefs in the future.

Going to the local bookstore can be very helpful. There is such a major selection of books, magazines, and CDs to choose from in order to determine which ones are best suited for them.

If you wish to save money on buying books and different forms of media, get a library card and you can go to the nearest library to browse. In turn, you can see what is available and decide what is the most appealing. One can reserve a book, a magazine, or a CD and pick it up at the local library.

Another option to consider is that many libraries have websites so you can see which books, magazines, and CDs are available to "check out" electronically. Then these items can be downloaded on a technological device for a specific time period, just as is normally done when going to the library. Such a method may be desirable, especially when parents and kids have very busy schedules or when kids have to check out library materials for school assignments.

One way to learn more is to focus on critical thinking activities in the home. For example, playing board games like checkers and chess against other family members and friends, one can develop different strategies by determining moves of the other player or players. If children are not inclined to participate, playing some games by themselves or online with others on a technological device or from an app can be a very good alternative.

No matter who plays the games and how the games are played, the idea is to become fully involved in the game. Usually, that is not going to be much of a problem since many people are already almost "addicted" to their technological devices, specifically their smartphones. It is suggested that with kids, in particular, time limitations are imposed so that their lives are not consumed with games and in order for them to have quality time with their family as well as to complete all school assignments.

Another way to inspire critical thinking and coordination at the same time is to either begin learning to play a musical instrument or to advance with a musical instrument. You need to know how to read notes. You are using your mind, coordinating your fingers, and reading music so that you can make progress. It takes time to practice and to perfect your skills in reading and playing music. This is not to say that learning a musical instrument is going to be easy to do, because it will require patience. No matter how old a person is, the enjoyment of music can be the end result.

Having the ability to play music, children will be able to concentrate much better. They can perfect their ability to study better. They can learn much more and perhaps even earn higher grades. Music may also help to ease their minds from their responsibilities and stress that they may be experiencing. Adults as well can ease stress that they may be feeling due to their responsibilities and stress in their personal and professional worlds by playing a musical instrument.

The family may actually feel better with this set period of time during the day when they can release any negative energy that has been accumulating and focus on some activity that is inspirational and satisfying for them personally. It may be necessary to develop a schedule so that everyone in the family is able to have ample time to play their musical instrument and so that everyone respects their space, allowing them distance, meaning that everyone not playing is in other rooms or out of the home.

If playing music is not an option due to the expense of the instrument and the cost of musical instruction, it is then a good idea to begin or to continue developing a hobby of some kind. In this way, you can fully devote time to such an activity so that you can concentrate on something other than your normal responsibilities.

Another easy way to become better educated is to learn more about one's culture by exploring one's own city or town along with cities and towns in the surrounding areas. Going to national and state parks and museums can be a great way to explore.

Within the city or town as well as in the surrounding cities and towns, consult local websites to help make decisions as to what one's interests are and when places are open. It is also suggested that, in order to have a full appreciation of the diversity of life, one considers attending new festivals or events. In this way, one's horizons will be expanded. Even if the family chooses not to visit unique and previously unexplored places in person, at least they will understand that they exist. Perhaps, later on in life as adults, such places will be considered.

When you and others go out of town on vacations, whether local or long distance, these trips too can be very informative for all concerned, providing opportunities to meet different people and see different parts of these areas.

While it is good to eat and to drink at restaurants and cafés that the family normally enjoys, it is also a good idea to experiment by going to places that are not usually considered. After looking online at their menus, if available, or by inquiring at these eating establishments, the family can decide if they wish to enter and order different foods and drinks. It can be a "vacation" for one's typical taste buds. If the family decides to try these foods and likes or dislikes what they are offered, so be it. At least, they will have tried something new and they can make decisions accordingly as to whether to go there again or not.

Granted, if there are children involved, they more than likely wish to have fast food if it is available. It is a good idea to have a condition with that, namely, to require that the family go to different restaurants and cafés to see what kinds of foods are available there.

Attending age-appropriate plays and then discussing why you like or dislike them is a great way to have meaningful conversations. You can become much more aware of how others in the family think and feel, although you may or may not be surprised by everyone's perspective. It is also a very good idea to discuss why such plays were developed in the first place. In this way, one's perspective about life can be that much more enhanced by discovering how others interpret the world around us.

As spoken by Jaques in Shakespeare's *As You Like It*, "All the world's a stage." Indeed, the world has a lot to offer and to view. People can get a better appreciation of the world around them by venturing forth to experiment, to enjoy, and to determine what is to their liking or not. Thus, one's education is important in the school environment, although one can learn just as much in the world outside the school environment.

KEY IDEAS TO REMEMBER

- Learning is not restricted to the classroom.
- Chores at home can be a learning experience.
- Going to a library and to a bookstore can generate inspiration for new ideas.
- Playing games and playing musical instruments can help students develop critical thinking skills.
- Having a hobby can relax everyone.
- Exploring towns and cities can promote a better understanding of the world.

Chapter Fifteen

Mentoring

When one has acquired a skill, it is a wonderful feeling of accomplishment, although it is a good idea to continuously review and to learn more about your field of expertise. Indeed, you deserve to feel very confident about your work.

While it is quite gratifying to know something very well, being able to share this information with others truly can be mutually beneficial. Others can become just as knowledgeable in your field of study. They too can feel very confident. Perhaps they too can pay it forward to others after they have learned the information as well as you.

A legitimate question is: Is there a need for mentoring? Of course there is! People who are novices in any field can gain a lot of knowledge by reading books and looking online by doing Google searches. These can be very good resources, and there are people who can easily learn and absorb this information as quickly as it is given to them, but mentors can personally assist and even inspire those who are new to a field by sharing their expertise.

Many retired individuals find that they want to share the knowledge they have gained throughout the years and discover that they can offer very valuable assistance to others who are new or continuing in the same field by mentoring them, particularly in the fields of business and teaching. As a matter of fact, many mentoring techniques are similar to those applied in teaching young adults in school.

Once a retiree has made the decision to mentor someone professionally, a logical question to address is how to find the right place in order to help the right people. After having worked at a company, a person gains a lot of knowledge and experience. One possibility for mentoring is to see if you can help the person who has replaced you, or if you can become a mentor for a period of time to others with whom you have previously worked. This benefits the learners and the company. In turn, you will gain the satisfaction of having helped to make a difference for all concerned.

In this day and age of needing to do things quickly, many people are too busy to be helpful and people in the workplace can become overwhelmed, wishing that they had someone to guide them in the right direction by listening to them and answering their questions. Mentors truly can serve as the "soft shoulders," the people on whom they can rely, if and when they have questions.

So, how does one pay it forward? Here are some things to consider. Upon going through the appropriate channels of a company in order to become a mentor, it is always important to determine with mentees, and any other employees who will be affected, what are the most mutually agreeable times and places to meet and to learn on a regular basis. Exchanging contact information can be very helpful. Barring emergencies that can and do unfortunately happen, this will promote reliability and solidify the relationship.

An easygoing personality has a way of lessening any stress that learners may be experiencing and shows them that you can be calm and receptive to any questions posed. Oftentimes, depending on their personalities, individuals learning new information tend to be hard on themselves when they do not understand challenging material as quickly as they feel they should. It is at this point that it is vitally important to show patience with them so that they ultimately will be more patient with themselves. Of course, this may be easier said than done, but it is possible to change one's mindset with patience and understanding.

Having a sense of humor while sharing with others can be very helpful. You can laugh about your subject. You can laugh about yourself from what you attempted in the past with various results. They can possibly laugh about themselves. The result of showing your sense of humor and laughing can be a very good stress reliever for both of you during the teaching and learning process.

Being encouraging can also be a great attribute, especially if others wish to learn what you know, even if they are having difficulty. Showing confidence in their ability to learn the material will help them feel less stress and enjoy the process of learning.

Tact is exceptionally important when there is a perceived setback in terms of what they are learning. Learners will be more apt to listen attentively regarding what needs to be clarified when a mentor is sensitive to their feelings. After all, they wish to be accepted for who they are as individuals and workers who want to learn more from you.

Offering praise when warranted is a tremendous way to encourage learners to continue their endeavors, and understanding what has been learned and applied will truly generate a very good relationship between the two of you along with inspiring them to continue to do outstanding work now and in the future.

Being logical, going from the simple to the complex in the explanation of something, will help others to understand more readily. In this way, they will appreciate the systematic progression of what is being learned. It is also extremely important to review by asking questions after a certain amount of information has been taught to confirm that they are learning and are able to apply their new knowledge.

If they do not necessarily understand what is being presented, it is appropriate to give follow-up questions that can lead to more efficient learning. It should be made clear that if and when learners have questions, their questions deserve answers. It should not be a problem if they are inquisitive. If they are shy, it may take time for them to gain the confidence to ask questions. It is hoped that they will become more self-confident with regard to the information being learned.

A very good technique is to ask mentees at the beginning of your meetings if they have any questions regarding what they have learned and experienced since the last time you two met. In this way, they will know you are receptive to listening and answering their questions. If and when there is an issue in understanding a concept, this would be the appropriate time to provide the necessary information.

A unique way to help society in general is by helping reporters who are always seeking different people with different knowledge bases. A great resource online is Help A Reporter Out (http://www.helpareporter.com). Anyone who can supply the requested information is encouraged to share their knowledge for the sake of their readership. The subject areas include biotech and health care, business and finance, education, energy and green technology, entertainment and media, general subjects, high technology, lifestyle and fitness, public policy and government, and travel. If a reporter accepts your ideas, you may need to grant them permission to publish your quotes for their articles, along with supplying your contact information, in the event they have subsequent questions.

Another way to share ideas in society is by writing letters to editors of various publications regarding societal issues, especially if you have constructive, realistic ways that individuals can become better both personally and professionally.

With your expertise, if you have the time and the inclination to do so, you may wish to organize your ideas for a workshop or for a series of workshops on behalf of certain groups. Upon perfecting your ideas, you may wish to advertise by means of social media or in the general media in order to promote these workshops. Perhaps, as an extra enticement, you may wish to consider asking for donations designated to a charity of your choice, with the charity's representative being present to collect the donations.

The success of future generations will be based in large part on how the current generation regards and works with young adults. In turn, future generations can use or expand upon the knowledge gained that may be helpful for them and for others.

While the ideas presented thus far deal with helping others professionally, the following ideas are to help young adults personally. You may wish to contact local high schools to see if they have career centers. You can offer to talk with students who may be interested in your line of work. If you wish to consider this idea, it is best to check the high schools' websites to see if they do have a career center and to contact the career guidance counselors in order to discuss your ideas. You may also need to be fingerprinted and undergo a background check before you are allowed to present to students on a school's campus. If there are no career centers, you may wish to contact teachers in your area of expertise and offer them your services as a guest speaker to their students.

The website for mentoring is http://www.mentoring.org, and it can be helpful for people who are willing to become mentors to link up with the younger generation so that they feel they are being heard and respected. Perhaps many friendships can be the result.

Becoming a member of Big Brothers Big Sisters of America (http://www.bbbs.org) is another great way for you to contribute to the younger generation. After fulfilling their requirements, such as fingerprinting, you will be connected with young adults, oftentimes those from broken homes. You can meet with young adults on a regular basis, taking them to the library, to a bookstore, or wherever is mutually agreed upon, so that you can listen to them talk about their lives and give them feedback. In this way, they can feel validated, and you may develop some friendships that will last many years.

Ward halls that include kids may offer other opportunities to help young people on a one-to-one basis. These young adults are especially deserving of individual attention because they generally have had many traumas to deal with. If you are interested, please check your local county ward halls for details and guidelines.

As noted, respect will shine back onto you. Those who learn from you will honor you for yourself as an individual. In turn, you are making a significant difference in helping those of younger generations by giving them individual attention so that they can excel personally and professionally.

KEY IDEAS TO REMEMBER

- Sharing one's knowledge with the current generation will inspire an appreciation of what has been learned and will result in that many more innovations by the current generation.
- After retiring, there may be a time to want to help current workers.
- Mentoring requires being patient, humorous, encouraging, tactful, able to praise, logical, and willing to answer questions.
- http://www.helpareporter.com is another way to share knowledge.
- http://www.mentoring.org, http://www.bbbs.org, and ward halls are other great ways to help current generations.

Chapter Sixteen

The Endless Education

While having an education for yourself has been a gift and can benefit anyone wanting to learn from you, indeed, education is endless. There is always so much to learn and to enjoy.

If you are working, when time permits, it is always a good idea to be learning something new. It can be related to your trade, so that you can advance financially for your job, or your field of study can be chosen based on personal interest.

If you decide to study something new that is of interest to you, you may wish to go online to do some research as to all the different possibilities available. If you wish to go to a bookstore just to browse, there are endless ways to expand your horizons.

If you prefer to be a student for a change, it is then best to see what classes are available at adult schools, junior colleges, colleges, and universities, either locally or online. Then you may judge for yourself as to what is the most desirable for you and for your schedule.

If you enjoy reading and if you have a library card, going online or going to your local library can also offer you a multitude of books, magazines, and videos for your enjoyment and for your information, as previously mentioned.

It can be a lot of fun to join a book club. You and the other members can determine what kinds of books you wish to read. You and the others can determine how frequently you wish to meet after being realistic as to what everyone's personal and professional schedules are like.

After reading the books, members may decide to have their book club meetings at different people's homes, with everyone else bringing the food and the drinks while the host or hostess supplies paper plates, utensils, cups, and napkins. Alternatively, you may wish to eat and to discuss the books at the same person's home. Other book clubs may wish to conduct a progressive dinner, with salads served in one home, the main meal in another home, desserts in still another home, and finally the discussion of the books in yet another home.

If you and your friends enjoy viewing and discussing movies afterward, movie theaters provide a whole host of possibilities so that you can involve yourself in them. In recent years, many movie theaters offer dinners and even alcoholic drinks. Otherwise, you and others may wish to view movies at your home in order to save money. After viewing them together, you and your friends can discuss the various parts of the movies.

If you prefer to enjoy movies by yourself as a form of escape, for example, of course you are totally within your right to do so. This can be a way to immerse yourself in what you are viewing.

You may wish to go online to YouTube (https://youtube.com) where you can find thousands of videos for your entertainment and for your education.

Watching television shows that are personally interesting to you can provide an endless source of education and enjoyment.

Listening to radio stations, whether they have talk shows or music, can be very inspirational.

Enjoying podcasts can truly be very rewarding and enjoyable.

Having hobbies already in place is another way for you to expand your horizons and to fully immerse yourself on a regular basis. If you have not involved yourself in a hobby, this is a good time for you to do some research as to which hobby you may wish to pursue.

Another way to enjoy an endless education is to attend conferences, such as a TED conference. You can acquire more details at https://www.ted.com. You may wish to go to different cities in order to listen to speakers dealing with technology, entertainment, design, specific causes, and politics, for example, with the side benefit of enjoying other cities, whether you've visited them before or not.

Using your smartphone and downloading apps can be a way to enjoy any number of things, such as recreational and educational games.

Traveling to different communities, states, and countries can be very educational and pure fun so that you can immerse yourself in understanding and appreciating other areas of our world. If you prefer to do so, you may wish to read about them and then to visit them. In this way, you can be more informed about what you are going to experience and thus better able to appreciate your trips.

Your own family members and friends may inspire you to venture forth into new areas of consideration and inspiration because their perspectives are different from yours.

Although the above suggestions are limited in scope, these ideas are for your enlightenment and for your education. Being your own individual with your own likes and dislikes, you can easily consider many more options.

After having been a resource for your community, you most definitely deserve to enjoy involving yourself in activities for your own personal pleasure. Keeping the mind active, informed, and inspired helps a person to stay mentally alert and to maintain a much more positive outlook on life.

It is by valuing the various forms of families, the very basis of our global society, that they become role models for the understanding, the improvement, and the success of one's society both on a personal level and a professional level. It is hoped that this book has been a form of enlightenment and motivation to help you and your family within society.

KEY IDEAS TO REMEMBER

- Learning is limitless and doesn't need to be in the classroom exclusively.
- Being a participant in a book club can result in having fun with others while gaining insight into the perspectives of different people.
- Different media online, on television, and on the radio can expand one's interests and open one's mind.
- People are a fantastic educational experience.
- One's education and experiences will result in a more fulfilling life personally and can help in one's profession.

Suggested Resources

BOOKS

Donne, John. *No Man Is an Island*. New York: Random House, 1970.

Gracián, Baltasar. *The Critic* (Spanish edition). Seattle: Amazon Digital Services, 2011.

Hamilton, Boni. Chapter 10, "Leveraging Technology for Kinesthetic/Tactile Learning." In *Integrating Technology in the Classroom: Tools to Meet the Needs of Every Student*. 1st ed. Eugene, OR: International Society for Technology in Education, 2015, 179.

Hinckley, Gordon B. *Standing for Something: 10 Neglected Virtues That Will Heal Our Hearts and Homes*. New York: Three Rivers Press, 2001, 49–53.

Korgan, Grant. *Two Feet Back*. Reno: Lucky Bat Books, 2012.

Price-Mitchell, Marilyn. *Reframing Success: Helping Children & Teens Grow from the Inside Out*. Creative Commons Attribution-NonCommercial-NoDerivs, 2013. https://www.scribd.com/document/325736590/Reframing-Success-Price-Mitchell.

Reeve, Christopher. *Nothing Is Impossible*. New York: Random House, 2002.

Shakespeare, William. *As You Like It*. New York: Simon & Schuster, 2004.

Stock, Gregory. *The Book of Questions*. New York: Workman, 1987.

———. *The Kids' Book of Questions*. New York: Workman, 2004.

PERIODICALS, MAGAZINE ARTICLES, JOURNAL ARTICLES, AND ONLINE JOURNALS

García-Carrión, Rocio, and Lourdes Villardón-Gallego. "Dialogue and Interaction in Early Childhood Education: A Systematic Review." *REMIE: Multidisciplinary Journal of Educational Research* 6, no. 1 (2016): 51–76. http://doi:10.17583/remie.2016.1919

Hendricks, Clara. "Children and Technology: Ten Ways to Help Parents Navigate Technology with Children." *Association for Library Service to Children (A Division of the American Library Association)* 13, no. 2 (2015): 36–37. http://dx.doi.org/10.5860/cal.13n2.36

Hille, Katrin, Kilian Gust, Ulrich Bitz, and Thomas Kammer. "Associations Between Music Education, Intelligence, and Spelling Ability in Elementary School." *Advances in Cognitive Psychology* 7, no. 1 (2011).

McDaniel, Brandon T., and Sarah M. Coyne. "Technology Interference in the Parenting of Young Children: Implications for Mothers' Perceptions of Coparenting." *Social Science Journal* 53, no. 4 (2016): 435–43.

Mikelić Preradović, Nives, Gordana Lešin, and Mirjana Šagud. "Investigating Parents' Attitudes towards Digital Technology Use in Early Childhood: A Case Study from Croatia." *Informatics in Education* 15, no. 1 (2016): 127–46.

Monson, Thomas S. "Hallmarks of a Happy Home." *Ensign Magazine* (October 2001): 3.

Rosen, Larry D. 2004. "Understanding the Technological Generation Gap." *The National Psychologist* (March–April 2004). Accessed May 15, 2017. http://www5.csudh.edu/psych/tnp45.htm

Todorov, Alexander, and Jenny M. Porter. "Misleading First Impressions: Different for Different Facial Images of the Same Person." *Psychological Science* 25, no. 7 (May 27, 2014): 1404–17.

Willis, Janine, and Alexander Todorov. "First Impressions: Making Up Your Mind After a 100-Ms Exposure to a Face." *Psychological Science* 17, no. 7 (July 2006), 592–98.

MOVIES

The Gift. DVD. Written and directed by Joel Edgerton. Burbank: Universal Studios, 2015. Featuring Jason Bateman, Joel Edgerton, and Rebecca Hall.

Room. DVD. Directed by Lenny Abrahamson. Santa Monica: Lionsgate, 2016. Featuring Brie Larson, Jacob Tremblay, and Joan Allen.

WEBSITES

Academic Pentathlon. Orange County Department of Education, Costa Mesa, CA. http://www.ocde.us/pentathlon

Big Brothers Big Sisters of America. http://www.bbbs.org

Chirban, John T., PhD, ThD. "Trust for Children of Divorce." *Psychology Today*. https://www.psychologytoday.com/blog/age-un-innocence/201610/trust-children-divorce

Christianson, Cassy. "How Your Child's Sensory System Develops." Ability Path. https://abilitypath.org/2014/06/08/how-your-childs-sensory-system-develops/

"Culture." Merriam-Webster.com. Accessed October 12, 2016. http://www.merriam-webster.com/dictionary/culture

Dewar, Gwen. "Music and Intelligence: Why Music Training, Not Passive Listening, Is the Focus of Recent Interest." *Music and Intelligence: A Parent's Evidence-Based Guide* (2008–2014). ParentingScience.com. http://www.parentingscience.com/music-and-intelligence.html

Dictionary. http://www.dictionary.com

Facebook. https://www.facebook.com

FaceTime. http://www.itunes.apple.com/us/app/facetime

Free Rice. http://www.freerice.com

Ginger Software. http://www.gingersoftware.com

Grammar Check. http://www.grammarcheck.net

Help A Reporter Out (HARO). http://www.helpareporter.com
Hungry for Music. https://hungryformusic.org/
I Can Help. http://www.icanhelpline.org
ISBN. http://www.isbn.nu
Leiner, Barry M., et al. "Brief History of the Internet." Internet Society. Retrieved May 24, 2017. http://www.internetsociety.org/internet/what-internet/history-internet/brief-history-internet
McKay, David O. *Family Home Evening Manual.* (LDS: Council of the Twelve Apostles, 1968), p. iii. Retrieved October 21, 2016. https://www.lds.org/manual/doctrine-and-covenants-and-church-history-student-study-guide/the-worldwide-church/president-david-o-mckay-no-other-success-can-compensate-for-failure-in-the-home?lang=eng
Mentoring. http://www.mentoring.org
Polish My Writing. http://www.polishmywriting.com
Quizlet. http://www.quizlet.com
Rate My Teachers. https://www.ratemyteachers.com
Semester at Sea. https://www.semesteratsea.org
Skype. https://www.skype.com
Society for Personality and Social Psychology. "Even Fact Will Not Change First Impressions." ScienceDaily. Accessed January 25, 2017. https://www.sciencedaily.com/releases/2014/02/140214111207.htm
Spelling School. http://www.spellingschool.com
TED. https://www.ted.com
United States Academic Decathlon. http://www.usad.org
Wikipedia. https://www.wikipedia.org
WyzAnt. https://www.wyzant.com
YouTube. https://www.youtube.com

About the Authors

Dr. Rex A. Holiday earned his doctorate in educational leadership with an emphasis in e-learning, and his professional interests are STEM research, curriculum development, instructional design, critical thinking theory, and quantitative reasoning. He is a reviewer, an editor, and a referee for several education research journals, a National Science Foundation review panelist, and a former school board trustee.

Steve Sonntag, MA, has been a mentor teacher, his district's high school teacher of the year, a language chairperson, a tutor, a workshop presenter, a participant in high school accreditations, and an author during the past forty-eight years. He emphasizes insight, hope, and inspiration to students, families, and teachers.

www.ingramcontent.com/pod-product-compliance
Lightning Source LLC
Chambersburg PA
CBHW020357100426
42812CB00001B/90